Christology Revisited

Christology Revisited

John Macquarrie

SCM PRESS LTD

Copyright © John Macquarrie 1998

0 334 02737 3

First published 1998 by
SCM Press Ltd
9–17 St Albans Place London N1 0NX

Typeset by Regent Typesetting, London
Printed in Great Britain by
Biddles Ltd, Guildford and King's Lynn

Contents

Preface

Let me begin by thanking the Rector and Faculty of Mundelein Seminary in the archdiocese of Chicago for the honour which they did me in inviting me to give the Albert Cardinal Meyer Memorial Lectures for 1998. This book contains the substance of these lectures, with some additional material.

The title given to the series and to the book, *Christology Revisited*, needs a word of explanation. In 1990 I wrote a book, *Jesus Christ in Modern Thought*, in which I tried to put together the results of many years of teaching and study in the field of christology, paying special attention to the difficulties which have been felt since the time of the Enlightenment in acknowledging Jesus Christ as the God-man.

But, like most authors, as soon as the book was finished and fixed in print, I began to realize that some things that might have been said had not been said, that many things could have been said better, while still other things should perhaps not have been said at all. So I feel the need to go back and revisit christology, and I believe that as long as there are Christian theologians, they will still be revisiting christology and seeking better understandings of what Kierkegaard called the 'absolute paradox' of the God-man.

In Chapter 1, I highlight some of the most important aspects of the paradox. Chapter 2 considers critically some ideas which originate in the New Testament itself, and which, I believe, have obscured the genuine humanity of Jesus Christ. In Chapter 3, we attempt to evaluate some ideas that had their beginnings around the time of the Council of Chalcedon, and have persisted in the church ever since. In Chapter 4, we turn our attention to the other side of the paradox and examine various views that have been included under the imprecise term of 'adoptionism'. Chapter 5 attempts to ease some of the difficulties by calling for a broader epistemology, in which interpersonal knowledge and self-knowledge are given their due alongside objective knowledge. Finally, in Chapter 6, we follow up some clues from Pascal, Berdyaev and Bonhoeffer in quest of the 'metaphysical' Christ.

Christ Church, Oxford 1998   John Macquarrie

I

The Absolute Paradox

In the Letter to the Ephesians, Paul (or one of his disciples) writes of his vocation to 'preach the unsearchable riches of Christ' (Eph. 3. 8). If christology is the study of the person of Christ, the attempt to answer the question, 'Who is Jesus Christ?', and if the riches of Christ are 'unsearchable', then the task of christology is one of extreme difficulty, perhaps an impossible one, certainly one that will never be completed. So generation after generation of Christian theologians revisit christology to wrestle anew with the problem. Sometimes it seems that a breakthrough has been achieved, as for instance at the Councils of Nicaea and Chalcedon. But on such occasions it soon becomes clear that the alleged 'breakthrough' has left unanswered questions, and these have to be taken up again. What is the case in the history of theology is replicated in the experience of each individual theologian who enters the field of christology. Wittingly or unwittingly, he or she has engaged on a quest to which it will be necessary to return again and again.

My earlier book on christology, *Jesus Christ in Modern Thought*, had been intended as the completion of a trilogy, which began with *In Search of Humanity*, continued with *In Search of Deity*, and was to end with a study of the coming together of humanity and deity in Jesus Christ. But our neat

schemes for handling theological questions are rarely able
to contain the realities with which they deal. So when I
came to write the third volume of the trilogy, I decided that
my scheme was too abstract, and that the question I must
try to answer was the concrete one raised by Dietrich
Bonhoeffer as he lay in prison just about a year before he
was hanged by the Nazis. In a letter to a friend, he wrote
that the great question agitating his mind was, 'Who is Jesus
Christ for us today?'.[1] This is a question that any one of us
might ask in this secular age, for the Christianity that was
for so many centuries the spiritual foundation of the
Western world has drastically declined. What significance
still attaches to Jesus Christ? Bonhoeffer, it is true, was
living at a time when the civil power was bitterly and
openly opposed to the church, and he himself felt com-
pelled to resist the civil power. But although today, both
in Germany and in other Western countries, the open
persecution of Christianity has come to an end, a deadly
indifference is widespread. Though for different reasons,
the existential question 'Who is Jesus Christ for us today?'
is as real and oppressive for us as it was for Bonhoeffer. For
a great many people today, Jesus is little more than a distant
figure of the past, and they cannot believe that he has anything important to say to the contemporary world. Such
people sometimes emphasize his irrelevance by referring to
him contemptuously as a 'Galilean peasant', though in fact
the records tell us he was a *tekton* or skilled craftsman (Mark
6. 3) and his exchanges with the Pharisees indicate that
he had been educated in the history and traditions of his
people and in the methods of debate prevailing at that time.

The very form of Bonhoeffer's question – 'Who is Jesus
Christ *for us today*?' – implies that in different times and in
different situations different ways of thinking of Jesus

Christ and different ways of expressing the thought may be required. This may well be true, and it is a point of which preachers and theologians have always taken account. The Lectureship in memory of Cardinal Meyer specifically directs that the lecturer should pay attention to the relation of theology to culture. From the very beginning, the church's attempts to express its beliefs concerning Jesus Christ have been couched in the language and ideas of whatever the prevailing culture happened to be. In the very earliest period, the gospel was preached in the context of Jewish messianic expectations, and Jesus was proclaimed as the Christ, the One anointed by God to be the Saviour of his people Israel. Very soon, in the wider context of Hellenistic culture, quite different categories were used. For most people the word 'Christ' no longer carried theological connotations but had been reduced to a proper name, and in the famous Chalcedonian Definition of 451, Jesus Christ was set forth in the Greek philosophical terminology of 'person' (*hypostasis*), 'nature' (*physis*) and 'substance' (*ousia*), a way of understanding him which had moved very far from the modes of thought found in the New Testament. The christology worked out in patristic times attained a classic status, and is indeed still the norm today.

But since the eighteenth century at least, that classic expression of the church's belief about Jesus has made little contact with the modern mind. It speaks the language and employs the conceptuality of a former age. However liberating that language may have been when the Christian message had burst out from Judaea into the wider world, it is not liberating in the modern age, but has become almost a barrier to understanding. So we in our time have to look for ways of communicating faith that will speak to the mentality of our contemporaries, just as the fathers of Chalcedon did in their time.

Immediately, however, we are faced with a danger that lies in Bonhoeffer's question. It asks about the meaning of Jesus Christ *for us today*, as if 'we today' constitute an especially important and privileged segment of humanity. Are we slipping into a kind of relativism, in which Jesus Christ is deprived of his objective reality and is allowed to be only what different historical or cultural groups can accommodate within their varying perspectives? We live in an age when relativizing has become popular. There is the danger that truth itself may disappear, for we are told that there are only opinions of different groups who are historically and culturally conditioned to believe as they do. But those who make such claims never apply these sceptical principles to their own views, which ought also to be treated as mere opinions, produced by historical accidents and having no better claim to truth or to be believed than the opinions they criticize. The sociologist Peter Berger may well have been correct in saying that 'it is sociological thought, and, most acutely, the sociology of knowledge, that offers the specifically contemporary challenge to theology'.[2] But he went on to say: 'Once we know that all human affirmations are subject to scientifically graspable socio-historical procedures, [the question remains] *which affirmations are true and which false*?'[3] He also pointed out that although extreme relativizers have in fact abolished the notion of truth, they implicitly claim truth for their own views.

I hasten to say, however, that I do not think that Bonhoeffer himself was tending toward the relativism I have described. For him, Christ was the 'centre', a point to which I shall come in a later chapter. His position was

probably not very different from that of Karl Rahner, who
gives a strictly theological reason for the revising of
dogmatic formulae. He writes: 'The clearest formulations,
the most sanctified formulae, the classic condensations of
the centuries-long work of the Church in prayer, reflection
and struggle concerning God's mysteries: all these derive
their life from the fact that they are not end but beginning,
not goal but means, truths which open the way to the ever
greater Truth.' He specifically includes the Chalcedonian
Formula in his remarks, and sees the need for restatement
not just in 'the transcendence of the mind which appre-
hends it' but in the dynamic of the truth itself which is
always drawing us into deeper truth.[4] We do indeed have a
peculiar interest in the significance of Jesus Christ *for us
today*, but we must not let that narrow perspective prevent
us from appreciating what earlier generations of Christians
were enabled to learn of the truth of Christ in their times.
In particular, in spite of differences in language and conceptuality encountered in any ancient document, we have to
enter into what has been called its 'governing intention' and
ensure that whatever was of importance in that intention is
preserved and passed on in any new formulation.

These brief remarks on the conflicting pressures of tradition on the one hand and the need for new formulations on
the other draw our attention to a dialectic which recurs
through all theology and particularly pervades christology,
so that sometimes one has the impression of trying to
square the circle. This phenomenon is the coincidence of
opposites (*coincidentia oppositorum*) of which Nicholas of
Cusa wrote and which he believed to be characteristic of
God himself. In a coincidence of opposites, which we might
also call a 'paradox', we find ourselves situated between two
truths which appear to be incompatible, yet each of which

appears to have a powerful claim. We cannot simply dismiss the one and retain the other, yet we may not be clear about how they can be reconciled. An obvious example is provided by the apparently conflicting claims that Christ is human, and Christ is divine (this was called by Kierkegaard the 'absolute paradox'[5]). From this basic opposition, others flow in quick succession. In method, does one begin 'from below', as it is popularly expressed, that is, from the human Jesus; or 'from above', from the eternal Word? Does one stress the temporal career of the historical Jesus, or does one look beyond to the metaphysical Christ? Where do we get our knowledge of Jesus Christ – from the testimony of the past or from present experience? And if we can only say, 'from both', we still have to decide what weight to give to one or the other.

These are only some of the tensions which are theologically rooted and which have been there since the beginning of the Christian church. And as we wrestle with them, we are constantly aware of that tension that pervades all of them, the tension from which we set out and which we found in Bonhoeffer's question: 'Who is Jesus Christ for us today?' How can we, the inheritors of the Enlightenment, who know (or, at least, have some knowledge of) evolution, genetics, the expanding universe, the constraints of history and so on, find any interest in the story of a 'marginal Jew',[6] a wandering teacher of two millennia ago, who performed miracles, was acclaimed as a Saviour figure, was crucified but then rose from the dead and ascended into heaven? Is there not an uncrossable gulf here, so that it is hardly an exaggeration to say that he and we exist in different worlds?

But it would be a sad state of affairs if we said that communication was impossible or that we could learn nothing from Jesus. That would be tantamount to denying that there is a common humanity that we share with people of all cultures, past and present, and would rule out hopes for any genuine peace and understanding among the races and nations of humankind. Some people who talk of 'cultural relativism' come close to this, as when they tell us that the cultural differences between ourselves and the people of the New Testament are so great that their world must remain virtually closed to us.

Certainly one cannot deny that the gulf is a wide one. But is it true, as Albert Schweitzer once wrote about Jesus, that 'he passes by our time and returns to his own'?[7] After all, in spite of what he said, Schweitzer was touched by Jesus to the very core of his being, and became an outstanding modern disciple. Apparently it was the story, full of Jewish mythology, of the beggar Lazarus lying outside the gate of the rich man (Luke 16. 19–31) that so impinged on Schweitzer that he gave up his comfortable lifestyle in Europe to found his hospital for 'Lazarus' in Africa. If we have the patience, the energy and the humility to study the New Testament we can still hear the message of Jesus; it can make us dissatisfied with ourselves so that we look for something better. If a European or a North American travels today to Japan or China, he or she is at first bewildered by all the barriers to communication – language, both in its spoken and written forms, manners and customs, even ideas of right and wrong in some areas of behaviour. The visitor from the West thinks at first that it will be impossible ever to get through these barriers. Yet if the effort is made and time is given to it, it is amazing how friendships can be formed and how one begins to under-stand the reasons behind customs which at first seemed bizarre. We need not think of culture as a fate which must rigidly determine our thinking and our aspirations. We are all formed by the cultures into which we are born, to a greater extent than we realize, because the influence is so pervasive that it is like the air we breathe and we do not notice it. But it is not the whole or the only determining feature in human life. There is a recognizable 'human nature' that is more fundamental than the cultural forms by which it is moulded. Given the will, barriers can be crossed and there are common human concerns that can unite those coming from both sides.

There is something more than that. In every culture, there sometimes appear strong-minded persons who are able to criticize and transcend the limitations of the intellectual and moral environments into which they were born. Such were Socrates, Shakespeare, Tolstoy and others, and such were great moral reformers. Their words and deeds have reached the minds and hearts of people far distant from themselves in space and time and manners. Such universal human beings have been few in number, but there have been countless other unknown persons who have formed friendships and built understanding across racial and ethnic boundaries.

Jesus must be counted as the outstanding example of a human being who has attracted a world-wide following and founded a world-wide communion. He did have culturally conditioned beliefs about causality, disease, the agency of angels and demons and so on, but these did not and do not obscure his central convictions, which he expressed in both word and deed – convictions concerning the sin that disfigures human life, concerning the righteousness necessary for the health of society, concerning above all the love in which human life is brought to its highest pitch of fulfilment. In those supremely important matters, he comes across to us clearly.

In this book, I intend to take up some of the paradoxes or conjunctions of opposites that we encounter in thinking about Jesus Christ. I do not think a time will ever come when theologians will no longer have to 'revisit' christology. Only God himself, we may believe, can have a fully adequate comprehension of the mystery of incarnation. For human beings, there will always remain inadequacies – the exaggeration of one side at the expense of the other, the confusion and mixing of what needs to be kept separate, fixation on a particular formula from which we need to be set free, and so on.

There are clearly limits as to how far we can go in the quest for understanding. I do not think that, if we remain Christian, we can ever escape the fundamental paradox, that Jesus Christ is both human and divine. There are no devices that would eliminate it, short of the destruction of Christianity itself. It will not do, for instance, to say that Jesus Christ is indeed human, but not divine. Many people have believed that, and many still do. Some of them would go further, and say he was a very great man, a very good man, even the most sublime human being that has ever lived. But they stop short at the idea that he was the Word of God incarnate, as the Christian church has claimed. But if that claim is denied, then Christianity collapses. Jesus Christ might remain as an inspiring moral teacher, to be set alongside Socrates and Confucius, but he could not be a Saviour or Redeemer, he could not be preached as the Lord who demands the ultimate allegiance of the believer, and it would be nonsensical to baptize people into his name or to celebrate the eucharist. Jesus Christ is indeed fully and truly a human being, but Christians from the earliest days have believed that there was something 'more' to him, though this 'something more' is very hard to define. It is what Paul meant when he said 'God was in Christ' (II Cor. 5. 19) or what Matthew meant when he spoke of Jesus as 'Emmanuel' and interpreted the title as 'God with us' (Matt. 1. 23). So what is this 'something more' that marks Jesus off from the rest of the human race, but without separating him? Or to put the question in another way, how close is he to 'ordinary' men and women, and how distant?

During the long course of Christian history, there have been other people who have tried to avoid the paradox by taking a different short cut. They have said that Jesus was indeed a divine being, but that he only appeared to be a man. He looked like a man, he talked like a man, he even suffered like a man, but that was only appearance. In reality, this was God dressed up like a human being, flitting briefly across the pages of human history. Some people were saying this in the very early days of the church, and they were called 'docetists', from the Greek verb *dokein*, 'to seem', for they thought that Jesus was a supernatural being who only seemed to be human. But if this belief were accepted, then once again Christianity would collapse. Jesus' whole career would be reduced to a pretence, even a fraud. Unless he has truly and fully lived in the human condition, he can have nothing to say to us human beings. He would be an alien existence from another world and quite irrelevant to us children of earth. So we cannot get away from the paradox of the one Person who is both human and divine. We have rather to stretch our minds as far as they will go to show that this is indeed a paradox and by no means nonsense or mere contradiction.

As Schleiermacher pointed out, there are two basic heresies relating to the person of Jesus Christ, and each of them destroys his significance for Christian faith. If we assimilate him too closely to the common human condition, then he is in the same boat with the rest of us, and cannot be the Redeemer. If on the other hand we make the difference between him and ordinary men and women limitless, a difference of kind, we cut ourselves off from him, and again make impossible the saving relationship. The task of christology is to find the right balance.

One difficult decision has to be taken right away. Where do we begin? If Jesus Christ is indeed the God-man, 'recognized', in the words of Chalcedon, 'in two natures, without confusion, without change, without division, without separation, the distinction of natures being in no way annulled by the union, but rather the characteristics of each nature being preserved and coming together to form one person and subsistence, not as parted or separated into two persons, but One and the same Son, God the Word, Lord Jesus Christ': if all this is the case, then we have a choice. We can begin our attempt to fathom the mystery of the God-man either from the human side or the divine side, either 'from below' or 'from above', to use that popular but not entirely satisfactory terminology which we noted earlier. Both approaches are to be found in modern theology, but I myself have opted for the humanistic approach, the one that begins from the human Jesus. At least since the time of Schleiermacher, this humanistic approach has been gaining ground in christology, though sometimes it has evoked powerful resistance: for instance, from Kierkegaard in the nineteenth century and from Barth in the twentieth. Of theologians of recent times who have followed the path 'from below', one could mention among Roman Catholics Rahner and Schillebeeckx, among Anglicans Knox and Robinson, and among Protestants Baillie and Pannenberg. In the long run, however, one finds that both approaches have strong claims and each needs to be supplemented by the other. To begin from the human Jesus does not mean that one ends with what is sometimes called misleadingly a 'mere man' (*psilos anthropos*).

But what then are the grounds for choosing the humanistic approach rather than the other? Harking back to Bonhoeffer's question about 'us today', if Christian theologians want to address the man or woman of today, they must take account of the fact that contemporary society in the Western countries has become so secularized and God has been so much left out of account in the lives and thinking of modern Western human beings that if anyone speaks of Jesus Christ as the God-man or the Son of God or in similar terms, this situates him in such a distant territory that many who hear such talk will immediately conclude that Christ is irrelevant to them. So for today's educator or preacher or interpreter, the practical issue of how to engage with a largely godless world directs such a communicator to the approach from below. Even people who say they are not interested in the question of God, or that they can attach no meaning to language about God, are surely interested in the question of humanity and the welfare of humanity, if they are serious at all. So how else can the communicator begin, if not with the humanity of Christ? And just as we saw earlier in discussing Rahner's call for the re-expression of ancient formulae, so again we may note here that what at first may seem simply a practical question also has a theological dimension. The very idea of incarnation implies that God meets people where they are, that he even condescends to come into human history and meet men and women in the midst of their human affairs. So the humanistic approach, provided it is not applied in an exaggerated or doctrinaire way, can claim to be justified on both practical and theological grounds.

I think that one may make the further point, that in the history of theology, although at least lip service has been paid to the full humanity of Jesus Christ, it has been overshadowed and minimized in so many ways that one might almost say that a kind of unconscious docetism has been at work since the earliest times. Attempts have sometimes been made to correct the imbalance, but they seem to make only a temporary impression. We all know the story of how the boy Luther grew up oppressed by the picture of Christ in the stained-glass window of his parish church. It was a picture of Christ the Judge, a Christ with little human sympathy. 'Luther,' we are told by a historian of the Reformation, 'shivered whenever he looked at the window, and saw the frowning face of Jesus, who, seated on a rainbow and with a flaming sword in his hand, was coming to judge him, he knew not when.'[8] But although Luther wrote at length and very feelingly on the humanity of Christ, he did not carry through his line of thought but developed the doctrine of a 'communication of attributes' (*communicatio idiomatum*) which, in defiance of Chalcedon, mixed together the attributes of humanity and divinity. So the present-day determination to do justice and to do justice consistently to the true humanity of Christ is a renewal of a long-standing desire among theologians to rectify an ancient imbalance. If the latest attempts to restore a clearer understanding of the humanity of the God-man sometimes lead to a new imbalance, we should perhaps be indulgent, for a move in this direction is long overdue and it would be surprising if some of the attempts to make it did not fall into distortion in the opposite direction. But finally, as I have been urging, both sides of the paradox must find adequate expression.

So in the following chapters I return first to the question

of the humanity of Jesus Christ and in particular to ways in which it has been compromised by various items in the traditional teachings of the church. I should not say or imply that it has been threatened by these doctrines themselves, but by certain interpretations or understandings of the doctrines. The doctrines I have in mind include the virgin birth or virginal conception of Jesus; the doctrine of *anhypostasia*, the belief still widely accepted among theologians, that although Jesus had a complete human nature, his personhood or *hypostasis* was that of the divine Word or Logos; various beliefs concerning the miracles of Jesus, his knowledge and his sinlessness. I want to make it clear that I am not proposing to deny or to advocate the abandonment of these doctrines and beliefs. But I would claim that they have to be very strictly defined and nuanced if we are to ensure that they do not undermine the teaching of Christ's true and full humanity.

The next step would then be to show that this fully human Jesus is not just arbitrarily selected from the human population but is, in a distinctive sense, the Christ of God or the Son of God or the Word incarnate, or whatever expression may be used to give voice to the church's belief that Jesus comes from God and is God's word to us. In spite of his political radicalism, Bonhoeffer was very orthodox theologically, as I will make clear in a later chapter. He believed that Jesus is the Christ or God-man in a sense which is in some way objective as well as subjective. He remarks rather sarcastically in one of his books that for German liberal theology (he had the Ritschlian school specially in mind) 'the Christ is Jesus declared divine by the community in a burst of enthusiasm. Jesus is Christ not in his nature and not in his person but in his effect on others.'[9] This sounds like an almost complete humanization of

Christ and of Christianity in general. Bonhoeffer, as we see, distances himself as far as possible from such a point of view. He remains committed to the Christian paradox, and I have argued above that the paradox cannot be dissolved without the destruction of Christianity itself. Bonhoeffer explicitly declares that rationality is more expendable than the paradox: 'In christology, the humanity of God and the divinity of man must be held together at the risk of destroying the rationality of the exposition.'[10] At a later point, we shall return to Bonhoeffer and his distinctive christology. But at the moment, I wish to draw attention only to what happens if the defence of Jesus' humanity is pushed to the length where his christhood is no more than the honour bestowed on him in a 'burst of enthusiasm' on the part of the Christian community.

The reduction of Christ and the Christian community in the way which Bonhoeffer describes is a form of a type of belief usually called 'adoptionism', and this has commonly been considered a heresy. I have myself been called an 'adoptionist', though I think unjustly. I think it is quite possible to begin the christological inquiry 'from below' without ending in adoptionism. But the threat that a humanistic approach to the christological question may lead to adoptionism is sufficiently serious that we must devote a chapter to the subject. Just what is adoptionism, and does it appear in a variety of forms? What is supposed to be heretical about it? Does it, like most heresies, contain elements of truth, and can these be salvaged even if we turn away from such elements of untruth as have found a place in this complex phenomenon? This chapter on adoptionism will alert us to the problems of a humanistic christology.

We continue the exercise in fine tuning by turning our attention to epistemological questions. What do we know concerning Jesus, and in what ways is such knowledge acquired? Clearly some of the questions are historical, but there is much more to this part of our inquiry than the history of Jesus Christ. It is almost universally recognized that anything like a full history of his career is unobtainable. Two thousand years after his birth the data are no longer accessible. Such records as we have – the books of the New Testament and a handful of allusions from other sources are small in quantity and even so leave enormous gaps – the so-called 'hidden years'. Moreover, there had already been a lapse of thirty or forty years between the death of Jesus and the earliest written Gospel, so the material available needs to be treated with the greatest care.

On top of that, the material in the New Testament is embedded in other material which is seeking to promote a religious understanding of Jesus, while the material from outside the New Testament comes from writers, such as Tacitus, who were openly hostile to the Christian move-ment. None of it is 'impartial' history, if indeed any history is impartial. But even supposing that the material were much more abundant and reliable than it is, would that in itself be helpful towards answering the really interesting questions about Jesus? Wittgenstein wrote: 'We feel that if *all possible* scientific questions were answered, the problems of life would still not have been touched at all.'[11] This general observation by the philosopher can be adapted to the problems concerning Jesus. If all possible historical questions were answered, the really interesting questions would remain. Kierkegaard in fact said something very similar in the nineteenth century. We can, with difficulty, get some historical information about Jesus, but that, in Kierkegaard's language, is 'knowledge'. Christ, on the other hand (making here a distinction between the human Jesus and the Christ of faith), is an object not of knowledge but of faith, and this is a different realm in which the historical knowledge has no relevance.[12] I do not agree with the very sharp disjunction which is made here between the historical Jesus and the Christ of faith, or that between knowledge and faith. But it is true that the really interesting questions about Jesus Christ are, for want of a better word, 'metaphysical' questions. So we have to ask about the range of human cognition. In our time, the ideal has been a purely objective knowledge, knowledge of facts, whether natural or historical. But surely there are other kinds of knowledge, and we diminish ourselves if we neglect them. What about knowledge of oneself, or knowledge of other people? What about knowledge of God, either in ordinary religious experience or in those more intense experiences which are called 'mystical'? Is love itself a kind of knowledge? Are belief and faith probes, so to speak, beyond established knowledge?

These questions prepare us for the final chapter on 'The Metaphysical Christ', what we mean when we speak of the divinity of Jesus Christ, his being as eternal Son and Word. Here we shall consider some of the New Testament passages which depict Christ in cosmic terms; some of the theologians and philosophers who have made the most far-reaching claims for Jesus Christ – Pascal, Kierkegaard, Berdyaev, Bonhoeffer; and some of the mystics – Dionysius, Bonaventura, Eckhart; and it will be necessary too to ask whether their claims are susceptible of an interpretation that will not deny value to the non-Christian religions of the world. Incarnation will still be a paradox beyond the powers of the human mind to resolve, but at least we shall have seen some of the compelling reasons that have led to the church's claims for Christ.

2

The Humanity of Jesus Christ

That Jesus Christ was a real human being who once existed on this planet is a proposition which, one might suppose, could hardly be doubted. But in fact, doubt has been cast on the proposition, in more ways than one. At the beginning of the twentieth century, a number of scholars constructed what were called 'Christ-myth' theories. In these theories, it was held that the figure of Christ was purely mythical, perhaps an amalgam from various myths of the ancient world, or possibly an imaginary saviour-figure produced out of the longings of the Roman proletariat. Such views have never gained much acceptance, for the evidence that Jesus really existed is too strong, though it is freely admitted by biblical scholars that the accounts that we have of Jesus are at some points legendary and at others expressed in mytho-logical ideas.

But the question that concerns us is not whether Jesus really existed, but whether he really existed as a truly human being. The fact that his story is entangled in legendary and mythological details and that he came to be acknowledged as the Son of God or the God-man seems to compromise his genuine humanity. Thus – as we have already noted – there were heterodox Christians in the early centuries who denied Christ's true humanity and considered him to be a super-natural being, and although the various 'docetic' and 'Gnostic' heresies were rejected by orthodox believers,

something of these heresies rubbed off even on the orthodox. Clement of Alexandria, for instance, though opposing
the gnostics, accepted their ideal of asceticism and believed
that Christ was sustained by divine power to the extent that
he was physiologically different from normal human beings
and did not need to eat, drink and digest in the ordinary
manner.[1] Yet surely one who differed so fundamentally
from ordinary men and women even on the fairly basic level
of how the body is nourished, kept alive and energized,
could hardly have been himself a human being. One would
have to say that this was a purely supernatural being who
manifested only an illusory appearance of humanity. The
docetists would be correct after all. But if the church
affirmed – and it had to affirm – that the One whom it proclaimed was the God-man or the incarnate Logos, then the
preachers and theologians of the church were constantly
walking the knife-edge of a paradox with a slippery slope on
either side. For they were constantly in danger of falling
into one or other of the two heresies described by Schleiermacher[2] – either of so entirely identifiying Jesus Christ with
the human race that he is completely engulfed in the human
condition and is therefore incapable of being a Saviour or
Redeemer, or else of so stressing his divinity and therefore
his difference from the human race that he is irrelevant to
the human condition and so once more has to be declared
incapable of being a Saviour or Redeemer. The closeness of
Jesus Christ to the whole human race and yet the decisive
difference is perhaps most clearly asserted in the following
words from the New Testament: 'We have not a high priest
who is unable to sympathize with our weaknesses, but one
who in every respect has been tempted as we are, yet without sin' (Heb. 4. 15). We shall come back to these words
later.

But we have to note that even in the New Testament itself there are passages which have been interpreted in ways which might seem to undermine the truth of his full humanity. Yet nothing could in fact suppress the memory that Jesus was known to the first disciples as a man of flesh and blood like themselves, so there are many unequivocal testimonies to his humanity. Though Mark, usually considered to be the first in time among the evangelists, makes much of the miracles attributed to Jesus and of what might be called the 'numinous' elements in his ministry, there is no doubt that a definitely human figure emerges. Near the beginning of his ministry, Jesus is tempted by Satan (Mark 1. 12); he is tempted again after Peter's confession at Caesarea Philippi (Mark 8. 33) and perhaps finally in Gethsemane (Mark 14. 35–36). This fact of temptation, which we encountered already in the verse quoted from the Letter to the Hebrews, is of vital importance to the genuine humanity of Jesus. He has known from the inside, as it were, the moral pressures to which human life is subject. Later we shall examine the problem in more detail, in a discussion of what we mean by the 'sinlessness' of Jesus. Here we are simply noting that already in Mark there is a frank acknowledgment that temptation entered into his experience, and of course the point is repeated by Matthew and Luke, who enlarge on Mark's account and tell us about the content of the temptations. Again, we note that Jesus prayed to the Father (Mark 1. 35), and the natural reading of the passages concerned suggest that like other human beings he was praying for God's help to face the difficulties of life. He accepted John's 'baptism of repentance for the forgiveness of sins' (Mark 1. 4, 9), and Mark, unlike Matthew, offers no apology for this, though it seems to conflict with the teaching that Jesus was sinless. But the two ideas are not in contradiction with each other, if we accept that Jesus was fully human and in such solidarity with his human brethren that he could represent them and repent on their behalf. Again, when someone calls him 'Good teacher', Jesus replies, 'Why do you call me good? No one is good but God alone' (Mark 10. 17–18). Mark's blunt reporting is changed by Matthew, who gives Jesus' reply as 'Why do you ask me about what is good?' (19. 17) and thereby deflects any suggestion that there could be a question of Jesus' goodness. Further evidences of Jesus' humanity are the attribution to him of the common human emotions, and in this Mark is followed by the other evangelists. He could be angry and upset, as when 'he looked around him with anger, grieved at the hardness of their hearts' (Mark 3. 5); and when he accused the Pharisees of hypocrisy (Mark 7. 6). Equally, he could conceive an impulsive affection for an honest questioner – 'Jesus looking upon him loved him' (Mark 10. 21). There was perhaps the deepest moment of emotion in the agony of Gethsemane, when he told the disciples, 'My soul is very sorrowful, even to death' (Mark 14. 34). The strength of this emotion at the beginning of the passion is intensified in Luke's Gospel, which speaks of 'his sweat as it were great drops of blood falling down to the ground' (Luke 22. 44). Though these words are believed by some modern critics not to have been part of the original Gospel of Luke, they are certainly very ancient and unquestionably testify to a firm belief in Jesus' true humanity.

I have concentrated attention on Mark's Gospel and the Synoptic parallels, but even the Gospel of John, which is sometimes claimed to present Christ as a predominantly supernatural figure, has moments in which the humanity of Jesus comes through clearly. We are told, for instance, that as he travelled through Samaria he was 'wearied with his

journey' (John 4. 6); and at a later time, when he came to
the sisters and friends of Lazarus and found them grieving
for the dead man, he himself was 'deeply moved' and wept
(John 11. 33–35).

It is interesting to note that in the earlier writings of the
New Testament the evidences of Jesus' essential humanity
are more clearly visible than in the later parts. This would
seem to show that the approach 'from below', as we have
been calling it, has a further argument in its favour, namely,
that it reproduces the progress of the earliest Christians in
their understanding of who Jesus is. But it has also to be said
that from the beginning or very near it, the disciples were
discovering that there is something 'more' in Jesus that
distinguishes him from the rest of the human race. Thus
in the Gospels there is a kind of alternation: sometimes
Christ's humanity is obvious, sometimes what for the
present I am calling simply the 'something more'. In the
famous words of Pope Leo I, 'Each nature in union with the
other performs the actions which are proper to it; the Word
those which are proper to the Word, the flesh those
which are proper to the flesh. The one is resplendent with
miracles, the other succumbs to injuries.'[3] I think one may
accept that Leo here correctly describes the pattern of the
Gospels, but fifteen hundred years after he wrote these
words, we may think that, like the Chalcedonian Definition,
they demand re-expression if they are to speak to the
modern age. Leo has drawn attention to the paradox and set
the two components of it side by side, he has recognized the
claims of both the divinity and the humanity in Jesus, but I
doubt if he has thrown light on the paradox.[4]

So now let us turn our attention to some elements in the
New Testament and in early dogmatic teaching which
direct us to the other side of the picture, and make us face

those characteristics in Jesus which distinguish him from the rest of humankind and which we associate with the acknowledgment of his divinity. Can we interpret these parts of the tradition in such a way that they can be seen not to contradict or abolish the humanity, but rather show us how that humanity, when raised to a certain level, its true and intended level, becomes a mirror or a transparency through which is imparted to us the reality of God, to the extent that our finite understandings are capable of apprehending it?

The first item to be considered here is the virgin birth or virginal conception of Jesus Christ. There is no mention of this in the earliest writings of the New Testament. The earliest writings of all are those of Paul, some of whose letters may have been written less than twenty years after the crucifixion: Paul has very little to say about the birth of Jesus Christ. The most important passage is this: 'When the time had fully come, God sent forth his Son, born of a woman, born under the law' (Gal. 4. 4). That verse seems to set Jesus fully and firmly within the human race. Like every other human being, he was 'born of a woman', and also like every other human being, he was born into a definite culture, 'born under the law', the most important feature of the Jewish people. This definite situating of Jesus within the human race and within a well-marked cultural and historical *milieu* is reinforced in the opening verses of Paul's most theological epistle, Romans. Here he refers to Jesus as '[God's] Son, who was descended from David according to the flesh and designated Son of God in power according to the Spirit of holiness by his resurrection from the dead, Jesus Christ our Lord' (Rom. 1. 3). There is nothing in these quotations from Paul to suggest that Jesus was conceived or born in any special way. Paul had no doubt that Jesus came from God entrusted with a mission of first-class importance both for Israel and for the 'Gentiles', the nations other than Israel. But it seems to me equally clear that Paul did not know of any virginal conception. Jesus was 'born of a woman' and 'descended from David according to the flesh', thoroughly human, yet this does not prevent Paul from affirming that he is 'Son of God', and when Paul goes on later to develop a christology, he can speak of Jesus as the 'new Adam'. Of course that word 'adam' is simply the Hebrew word for a human being.

Likewise Mark, composing his Gospel perhaps twenty years after Paul had written his principal letters, does not seem to know of anything special about the birth of Jesus. He begins his story when Jesus is already in his thirties, and the first major event in the story is Jesus' baptism by John.

A further period of fifteen or twenty years elapsed before the church had the Gospels of Matthew and Luke, at least, in their present form. So if, as both of these Gospels claim, Jesus was born in the reign of Herod the Great who died in 4 BCE, there must have been a period of eighty or more years between the birth of Jesus and the first surviving accounts of the birth. It is not unreasonable to think that any adults who had been living at the time of the birth and who knew anything about it must have been long since dead. It is also not unreasonable to suppose that Matthew and Luke, writing in retrospect and knowing all the subsequent history of Jesus' ministry, death and resurrection, and seeing around them the steady progress of the church, believed, rightly, as history has shown, that in some way that birth had been no ordinary birth but a turning-point in history. At that period in history, it was believed that the births of outstanding persons would be marked by some publicly observable phenomena. Matthew's Gospel tells of a special star appearing at the time of Jesus' birth and astronomers have tried to discover whether there was some unusual celestial object to be seen about that time, perhaps a comet or an unusually brilliant conjunction of heavenly bodies. Luke, on the other hand, tells of an appearance of angels to the shepherds. But what is of more interest to us is that both evangelists tell of a phenomenon that was not publicly observable, namely, a virginal conception. This is a tradition of a different kind, and we do not know its origin or how it was transmitted to the authors of the two Gospels which report it.

The story is different in each of the two Gospels, and it is impossible to know whether we have two independent traditions, or whether in the course of its transmission over quite a number of years the original tradition has assumed two distinct forms. In Matthew, the annunciation of the coming birth of the Messiah is given to Joseph by an angel who appears to him in a dream (Matt. 1. 18–25). In Luke, the annunciation is made directly to Mary by an angel and Mary gives her assent. How then do we understand this tradition, and what is its significance for the humanity of Jesus?

In the first place, we must try to get away from the idea that the story is primarily concerned with a biological miracle. It would in any case be difficult to know exactly how the evangelists understood that miracle. Our understanding of human reproduction today is vastly different from what people in the ancient world believed to be the case. There was no knowledge then of living cells which unite to form a new individual human being. The father was the *genitor* or begetter, the mother's role was the purely receptive one of sustaining, nourishing and eventually bringing forth the life that had been implanted within her. So even if today in the context of our modern scientific culture we were to think of anything so improbable to modern ears as a virginal conception, we would be understanding it in quite a different way from what was in the minds of the evangelists.

But when we get away from the biological level of thinking and try to understand the tradition in a purely theological way, we see that Matthew and Luke were grappling with the profound question of the origin of Jesus Christ. They were saying that the life that had been implanted in Mary had come from God. Jesus Christ is not simply the product of natural evolution nor even of human procreation – there is something 'more' in Jesus, something that Matthew recognizes when he connects the birth of the child with an Old Testament prophecy, 'Behold, a young woman shall conceive and bear a son, and shall call his name Immanuel' (Isa. 7. 14). This also connects with the title 'Son of God' as given to Jesus in the early church. The idea that the being of the child was derived from the father while the mother's role was receptive demanded that if Jesus is indeed 'God with us', then theologically God is his Father – a theological truth which, as we shall see shortly, eclipses any biological considerations.

Up to this point, we have considered what Paul, Mark, Matthew and Luke have said (or, as the case may be, have refrained from saying) about the virgin birth. We have still to consider John's Gospel. John also is silent about the birth of Jesus, but there are two passages in the Prologue to the Gospel which bear directly on the questions we have been discussing. The first passage is the opening verse: 'In the beginning was the Word, and the Word was with God and the Word was God' (John 1. 1). Here John says nothing about the birth of Jesus, nothing about any genealogy such as we find in Matthew and Luke, but goes back immediately to God. He simply brushes aside the circumstances of Jesus' birth and of his ancestral history – just as Jesus himself had brushed aside the question of his Davidic descent (Matt. 22. 41–45). For John, the something 'more' in Jesus is that he comes from God. The second relevant passage in the Prologue reads: 'But to all who received him, he gave power to become children of God; who were born, not of blood nor of the will of the flesh nor of the will of man, but of God' (John 1. 12–13). The second part of this quotation does seem to contain a reference to virginal conception, to a birth that is 'not of blood nor of the will of the flesh nor of the will of man but of God'. But what is interesting is that these words are applied not to the birth of Jesus himself but to the spiritual birth of those 'who received him, who believed in his name' and who have been made by him 'children of God'.[5] The language here seems to be connected with a later chapter in the Gospel where Jesus says to Nicodemus, 'Truly, truly, I say to you, unless one is born of water and the Spirit, he cannot enter the kingdom of God. That which is born of the flesh is flesh, and that which is born of the Spirit is spirit' (John 3. 5–6). Here the theological interpretation of the virgin birth is extended to those who have believed in Jesus. The individual Jesus is surrounded by a community which he has called into being, and together they constitute a new humanity, a new creation deriving from a new Adam, Jesus Christ, who realizes the intention of God where the old Adam had failed.

Among modern theologians, I think the one who has dealt most adequately with the doctrine of the virgin birth is Karl Barth. He has tried to enter sympathetically into the motives of the evangelists and has concentrated on the spiritual and theological significance of the doctrine. Barth is contesting the rather loose liberal conception (found, for instance, in D.F. Strauss) that God is incarnate in the whole human race. This may be a partial truth, but it takes away any distinctiveness from Jesus Christ. Barth writes, in criticism of such views: 'The passages in Matthew and Luke that are concerned with the earthly human origin of Jesus say, No! His earthly human origin is a mystery; it can be understood only as a unique and peculiar act of God.'[6] Further on, he writes: 'The virgin birth denotes particularly the mystery of revelation. It denotes the fact that God stands at the beginning where real revelation takes place – God, and not the arbitrary cleverness, capability or piety of man. In Jesus Christ God comes forth out of the profound hiddenness of his divinity in order to act as God among us and upon us.'[7] In his book on baptism, Barth extends some of these ideas to the Christian believer by claiming that 'when a man becomes a Christian, his natural origin in the procreative will of his father is absolutely superseded and transcended'.[8] I think enough has been said to show that the doctrine of the virgin birth of Christ can be interpreted in such a way that it does justice to the distinctiveness of Christ without infringing his genuine humanity, which would mean turning his distinctiveness within the human race into a disastrous separation from it.

Another problem is presented by the miracles ascribed to Jesus in the New Testament. If he was fully and truly human, how could he walk upon water or feed thousands of people with a few loaves? Do we not see here again a docetic attitude, which has transformed Jesus into a supernatural being? Great human figures, especially those who found religions, are made the subject of legends and we see the tendency at work in the stories told about Moses, Buddha, Krishna and many others. To the extent that Christians believe Jesus to have been a worker of miracles, do they not deny his true humanity? And in an age like ours, which is sceptical of miracles, does this not mean that Jesus can be written off as irrelevant to the human condition?

More than one reply can be made to these questions. I think we must first except the healing miracles from consideration. The first title that was given to Jesus once his distinctiveness began to be perceived was Messiah or Christ, the anointed One who would bring salvation to his people Israel. In Hebrew expectations, the Messiah would among other things be a healer. In the messianic age, 'the eyes of the blind shall be opened, and the ears of the deaf unstopped; then shall the lame man leap like a hart, and the tongue of the dumb sing for joy' (Isa. 35. 5–6). There are many reports in the Gospels of healings by Jesus, and there can be no doubt that these were the cause of his popularity in the early days of his mission. There can be little doubt either that he did in fact have a gift of healing. Some people in our time still have this gift, and even the most sceptical persons could hardly deny that such healings occur. But to explain them is another matter. The relations of body and mind are still not understood, though they are obviously relations of a most intimate kind. Perhaps such healings will be much better understood in the future, but neither then nor now does it seem necessary to suppose that the agent or instrument of such healings possesses magical or supernatural powers, though the gift which he or she exercises comes ultimately from God.

The serious problem arises not with the healing miracles but with the so-called 'nature' miracles. These would seem to imply that Jesus had the omnipotence of God, or, at least, powers far greater than those which belong to ordinary human beings. But there are good reasons for doubting whether any nature miracles were ever performed by Jesus. In the temptation narratives included in the Gospels of Matthew and Luke, Jesus seems to set his face against such miracles. In fact, they would have been quite inappropriate to the kind of mission on which he was embarking. One of the temptations was to throw himself down from the pinnacle of the Temple, and land unhurt at the bottom (Matt. 4. 5–7; Luke 4. 9–12). No doubt such a performance would have persuaded many people that this was indeed the Christ, but such a miracle had nothing to do with what Jesus conceived as his vocation. So he rejects the temptation, and at other times discourages people from looking for 'signs'. Spectacular deeds, though they might impress the ignorant, were not part of Jesus' methods.

So what do we say about those stories of walking on the lake or feeding thousands with a few scraps of food? We must reject their literal truth, not because of the sceptical temper of our age, but because Jesus himself rejected such actions and because they are incompatible with his true humanity. In addition, we Westerners have very literalistic, unimaginative, matter-of-fact mentalities. We find it hard to appreciate that truth can be conveyed in parables and allegories and even in myths and legends. Consider that story about Christ walking on the waters (Matt. 14. 22ff.) Taken literally, it would be a rather pointless story. But as an allegory, it has much to say. If people ask me, 'Did Jesus really walk on the sea?,' I reply, 'I've been walking myself on the water for quite a few decades. I've often been sinking, but like Peter I've found that faith keeps one afloat.' 'Walking on water' is a perfect description of the human condition, and the story of Christ walking on the water is not a story of his supernatural power but rather an illustration of how in his humanity he shared all the insecurity and vulnerability of our earthly life. As for the feeding of the multitude, if we look at the version of this story in John's Gospel (John 6. 1–14, 25–59), we see that it is followed later in the chapter by eucharistic teaching about the bread that comes down from heaven. This suggests that these stories of feeding large numbers of people with only a few pieces of bread and fish are allegories of the eucharist, where minimal quantities (in a physical sense) of food and drink convey the very life of Christ himself, his body and his blood.

Just as there was a tendency to ascribe, if not actually omnipotence, at least supernatural powers to Jesus in his earthly human life, there was a similar tendency to ascribe to him omniscience, or, if not full omniscience, at least supernatural knowledge. In at least one passage of the New Testament it is made clear that Christ's knowledge falls short of omniscience. Concerning the 'last day', Mark's Gospel quotes Jesus as saying, 'But of that day or that hour, no one knows, not even the angels in heaven, nor the Son, but only the Father' (Mark 13. 32). Luke suggests that Jesus, like other human beings, learned as he went along, and he writes, 'Jesus increased in wisdom and in stature, and in favour with God and man' (Luke 2. 52). The Letter to the Hebrews says, 'Although he was a Son, he learned obedience through what he suffered' (Heb. 5. 8).

But in other passages, it seems to be suggested that Jesus had knowledge of future events, for in Mark's Gospel, he makes predictions of his sufferings, death and resurrection, following on Peter's recognition of him as the Christ, and on his journey to Jerusalem (Mark 8. 31; 9. 31; 10. 32–34; 10. 45). Nowhere in the New Testament would we find support for the view, held by some Christian writers of earlier times, that even in the womb Jesus already knew that he was Messiah and knew the complete train of events through

which he would have to go. Such a view would utterly
demolish belief in his true humanity, and would therefore
demolish the doctrine of the incarnation. But even the more
limited but still supernatural knowledge of the future which
Mark attributes to him needs to be critically examined if we
are to safeguard that full humanity which belonged even to
the God-man.

Bultmann and other New Testament scholars have taken
the view that the predictions of his passion made by Jesus
were *vaticinia ex eventu*,[9] though that is perhaps going too
far. Certainly, Mark and the other evangelists were seeing it
all in retrospect, they knew all that was going to happen
when Jesus reached Jerusalem, and when they told the
story many years after the event, they may very well have
believed that things were much clearer to Jesus at the time
than they actually were. Obviously, he must have known in
a general way the risks that he was running in going up to
the capital city, the headquarters of those who were determined to destroy him. But this was a knowledge within what
is accessible with ordinary human resources, not a detailed
vision of the future which we would have to pronounce
supernatural. I think this point is proved by the fact that
even as late as those trying moments in the Garden of
Gethsemane, Jesus could still pray to the Father that the
cup he seemed fated to drink might be removed; yet his
prayer ends with the words, 'Not my will, but yours!' (Mark
14. 36).

However, in insisting on Jesus' humanity, we are not in
the least detracting from his stature but rather increasing it.

I think this truth has never been better expressed than it
is by the Catholic New Testament scholar, Raymond
Brown:

A Jesus who walked through the world, knowing exactly what the morrow would bring, knowing with certainty that after three days his Father would raise him up, is a Jesus who can arouse our admiration, but still a Jesus far from us. He is a Jesus far from a mankind that can only hope in the future and believe in God's goodness, far from a mankind that must face the supreme uncertainty of death with faith but without knowledge of what is beyond. On the other hand, a Jesus for whom the future was as much a mystery, a dread and a hope as it is for us, and yet at the same time a Jesus who would say, 'Not my will, but yours!' – this is a Jesus who could effectually teach us how to live, for this is a Jesus who would have gone through life's real trials. Then we would know the full truth of the saying, 'No man can have greater love than this, to lay down his life for those he loves' (John 15. 13), for we would know that he laid down his life with all the agony with which we lay it down.[10]

If someone asks, 'Are we saying then that Jesus is a mere man?', I would have to reply, 'What do you mean by a *mere* man?' Is not a man, a human being, the creature which God made in his own image and likeness (Gen. 1. 26)? Jesus in his humanity is the man who has fulfilled God's intention for the human race so that he is in Paul's words 'the image of the invisible God' (Col. 1. 15) and we have 'the knowledge of the glory of God in the face of Jesus Christ' (II Cor. 4. 6). His humanity is not abolished by the presence of God in him but is transfigured into a true humanity. For the first time we are shown what the potentiality of humanity really is.

Finally, something needs to be said about the sinlessness of Jesus. This is, according to the verse from Hebrews already quoted, what distinguishes him from other human beings. But it does not detract from his true humanity. It is, on the contrary, what makes him the true human being, for sin is not part of human nature but a violation of human nature. Human nature is, so to speak, the raw material out of which a human life has to be built. Human nature is not in itself sinful or sinless, for sin can arise only when the person, the leading edge of the self, chooses to adopt one desire or possibility of action over another. Sinlessness does not abolish humanity but brings it to the level God intended for it in the new Adam.

3

Two Traditional Ideas Evaluated

In the previous chapter, we considered those parts of the New Testament which have a bearing on the question of Christ's humanity. While we found that Jesus Christ does come across as a human being, though certainly a very 'special' one, we found it necessary to examine some ideas which might seem to put his humanity in question, especially the story of a virgin birth, the performance by Jesus of miracles, the apparently supernatural extent of his knowledge, the assertion of his sinlessness. All of these could be interpreted in ways that would compromise his full humanity, and they were so interpreted by the various docetic sects that were already coming into being in the first century. I tried to show, however, that these parts of the tradition can and, I believe, should be interpreted in ways that do not impugn the full and true humanity of Jesus Christ. But the tendency toward docetic interpretations continued and even gained strength in the period after the books of the New Testament had been written. For several centuries the church, both through councils and individual theologians, laboured hard to produce an adequate statement on the person of Jesus Christ. Sometimes his 'specialness', his peculiar relation to God the Father, was stressed in ways that obscured his humanity. But every action produces a reaction, in theology as in other areas, so that sometimes the desire to acknowledge the solidarity of Jesus with the human race led to a minimizing of his distinctive status. The pendulum swung back and forth, and no sooner was a solution of the problems reached than a new controversy would break out. About half way through his massive *History of Dogma*, Adolf Harnack declares (and one can almost hear a sigh of weariness): 'The hundred and one doctrines which floated around the trinitarian and christological dogmas were as fickle and uncertain as the waves of the sea.'[1]

But some of these dubious speculations did persist, and have not only lasted down to our own time, but have even acquired the reputation of being the 'orthodox' version of the faith. In this chapter I intend to consider two related doctrines concerning the person of Christ, usually called *anhypostasia* and *enhypostasia*. Both originated out of the christological debates of the fifth and sixth centuries, but they continue to reappear in new guises. It is common knowledge, of course, that the actual noun forms, *anhypostasia* and *enhypostasia*, were not used in the original controversies, but are inventions of later theologians. We should note that Bishop Kallistos Ware holds that it was not just a desire for convenience that led to the coining of these terms, but also the tendency of Western theologians to develop abstractions. But although ancient theologians and some modern ones may not actually use these expressions, the ideas underlying them have been and still are around, however they may be designated, and I think that they still constitute a danger threatening a true appreciation of Christ's humanity. Though we shall only get a clearer understanding of the meaning of these terms as the discussion proceeds, a preliminary indication is demanded. *Anhypostasia* (the word means literally the 'state of being

without a *hypostasis*') is the doctrine that although Jesus
Christ had two natures, a divine and a human (as Chalcedon
teaches), these 'concur' or are united in a single person
(*hypostasis*), and this person is the divine Logos, so that the
human *hypostasis* is superseded and replaced by the *hypostasis*
of the divine Logos. Jesus Christ therefore is without a
human *hypostasis*. *Enhypostasia*, a doctrine which arose later
as a modification of *anhypostasia*, concedes that Jesus Christ
did indeed have a human *hypostasis*, but it was taken up and
included in the *hypostasis* of the Logos. Thus baldly stated,
these notions are not only hard to understand, but it may be
even less clear how they can help us towards a better understanding of the God-man. Yet these are stages through
which the search for understanding has historically moved,
and we shall see that they are not irrelevant to the current
problems.

The best way to proceed is first of all to review the basic
vocabulary that was used in the fifth-century discussions of
christology. I do not think I exaggerate when I say we are
entering a conceptual jungle. Scholars have been sifting
though the terminology for centuries. The Chalcedonian
fathers themselves went quite a long way towards sorting
out the various terms and giving each its own specific meaning. They were striving to find a formula that would unite
the range of opinions found in different parts of the church,
and the Chalcedonian Definition must be accounted one of
the most truly ecumenical documents in the history of the
church. In R. V. Sellers' words, 'In a very real sense, the
Council of Chalcedon may be called the place where the
three ways (Alexandrian, Antiochene and Western) met.'[2]
A. Grillmeier is even more emphatic: '[In the Chalcedonian
formula] as in almost no other formula from the early
councils, all the important centres of Church life and all

the important trends of theology, Rome, Alexandria, Constantinople and Antioch, have contributed toward the framing of a common expression of faith.'[3] But although the work of the Council and the resulting formula are worthy of the highest respect, one may still wish to make some criticisms. Although much was done to bring order into the terminology, the different associations which a word might have in the minds of different people could not be immediately harmonized. In particular, if a term had been used at some time in the past by someone who had later been judged to be heretical, it was very difficult to rehabilitate that word.

There were three terms widely used in the christological discourse of that period: *ousia*, *physis* and *hypostasis*. At different times and in different contexts, these three terms had different meanings, but at other times and in other contexts, their meanings might overlap, and one might even think that they were synonyms. I was not exaggerating when I used the expression 'conceptual jungle'. Let us consider each of them.

1. *Ousia* is the broadest of these three terms. It was often translated into English as 'substance', but this was unsatisfactory for various reasons. In modern English, 'substance' is generally used for the material stuff out of which something is made, and occasionally it is used for property, as when we talk of a 'man of substance'. Such ideas are far from the christological use. A second objection is that 'substance' suggests something solid and unchanging. The basic meaning of *ousia* is better expressed by the English word 'being'. This point has been understood by liturgical revisers, so that in the Nicene creed, for instance, we now say of Jesus Christ that he is 'of one being' with the Father, rather than 'of one substance'. I understand 'being' as an

inclusive word, covering every aspect of the entity of which it is used – in the case of a human being, that person's body, mind, soul and whatever else belongs to a human existence. It is harder to say what is meant by the 'being' of God, though if we say that Jesus Christ is 'of one being' (*homoousios*) with the Father, we obviously have some idea of the Father's being in mind, as well as of Christ's.

2. *Physis* is generally translated into English as 'nature'. Like *ousia*, it is a word that has to do with existence. In fact, the Greek root *phy* is cognate with the English root *be*, and with many other words of similar meaning in the Indo-European family of languages. But here again the complaint might be made that this English word 'nature' is too static in its meaning to be a good equivalent for the Greek word. The notion conveyed by *physis* is that of 'becoming' or 'emerging', of 'coming to be' rather than of unchangeable being. This is important when we talk of Christ having two natures. If these natures were already fixed, then to say that someone had two natures might suggest the absurdity that the same creature could be both a dog and a cat simultaneously. In modern philosophies, it is acknowledged that 'human nature' is not, as was sometimes supposed, a constant always the same even in different cultures, but a nature that emerges or grows or transcends, though if it has these positive characteristics, it must also have the possibility of regressing and growing less. What we mean by a 'divine nature' is beyond our power to say, though the direction in which we must look is indicated by transcendence in human nature.

3. *Hypostasis* may be translated 'subsistence' in the sense of something that exists as a real individual entity in the world. The word is itself one with a very impersonal sound, a kind of technical or metaphysical equivalent to the

common word 'thing'. It was probably in Christianity that the word *hypostasis* was first used in the sense of 'person'. The word *prosopon* was also used, and appears in the Chalcedonian Definition as an alternative to *hypostasis* in the phrase 'one *hypostasis* or *prosopon*', but *prosopon* was the word commonly used for 'face' or even 'mask', and so carried a suggestion of superficiality which does not belong to *hypostasis*. It has been claimed that the equivalence in Christian thought between *hypostasis* and *prosopon* was an important step toward the modern concept of 'person' and was one way of saying that persons take precedence over things, or that persons rank more highly in the cosmic hierarchy than do things or animals. But this brings us back to the specific question for which this discussion of terminology has been a preparation. What would it mean to say that Jesus Christ did not have the constitution of a human personal being, but instead his personal being was that of the divine Logos? Could there be a 'nature' without a 'person' or, more precisely, a human nature without a human person?

Let me say first of all that it seems axiomatic that Jesus Christ could have only *one hypostasis*, for that means one self, one personal centre, one *hegemenikon* or 'leading edge', as I expressed it in an earlier writing.[4] If there were two personal centres, two wills, two leading edges or however we might put it, this would be a pathological condition, or it might mean that there were two separate Christs. But can it be any solution to say that Jesus Christ had no human personal centre, and that the place of this was taken in him by the divine Logos?

To understand more clearly what was at stake, we must go back to an acute controversy that was raging in the years before the Council of Chalcedon. Nestorius, the Patriarch of Constantinople at that time, was alleged (perhaps unfairly) to have made such a sharp distinction between the human Jesus and the divine Logos that he had broken up the unity of the Christ. The major opponent of Nestorius was Cyril of Alexandria. In the second of his letters to Nestorius, written in 430, that is to say, twenty-one years before the Council of Chalcedon, Cyril defended the unity of Christ's person in the following statement:

> We do not affirm that the nature (*physis*) of the Word underwent a change and became flesh, or that it was transformed into a complete human being consisting of soul and body; but rather this, that the Word, having in an ineffable and inconceivable manner personally (*kath' hypostasin*) united to himself flesh animated with a living soul, became man and was called the Son of Man, yet not of mere will or favour, nor again by the simple taking to himself of a human person (*prosopon*), and that while the natures that were brought together into this true unity were diverse, there was of both one Christ and one Son: not as though the diverseness of the natures was done away by this union, but rather the Godhead and Manhood completed for us the one Lord and Christ and Son, by their unutterable and unspeakable concurrence and unity . . . We must not then divide the Lord Jesus Christ into two Sons. To hold this will in no wise contribute to soundness of faith, even though some make a show of acknowledging a union of persons (*prosopon*). For scripture does not say that the Word united to himself the person (*prosopon*) of a human being, but that he became flesh. But this expression, 'The Word became flesh', is nothing else than that he became partaker of flesh and blood like us and made our body his own, and

came forth a man of a woman, not casting aside his being God, and his having been begotten of God the Father, but even in the assumption of flesh remaining what he was.[5]

This seems a clear enough statement of what is meant by *anhypostasia*, though in fairness to Cyril, it must be pointed out that he implicitly acknowledges that in speaking of incarnation, one is always dealing with a mystery that resists explanation. This is clear from the Patriarch's frequent use of such words as 'ineffable', 'inconceivable', 'unspeakable' and so on. But the main point that Cyril is making is obvious. Though Jesus Christ has two natures, he is a unitary person, and that person, in Cyril's view, is the person of the divine Logos, 'remaining what he was'. Whether this doctrine is a part of orthodox belief is not quite so clear. It is not explicitly stated in the formula of Chalcedon, but the letter of Cyril just quoted, together with the *Tome* of Pope Leo, was 'received' by the Council, and this implies approbation and associates these documents with the Council's decisions. The Council, Leo and Cyril appear to stand firmly together. 'Peter has spoken through Leo. This is the teaching of Cyril. Anathema to him who believes otherwise'.

But whether we think the doctrine of *anhypostasia* was intended to be part of the orthodox christology or not, it has surely to be rejected as undermining the true humanity of Christ.

I venture to say this for a variety of reasons. First, Cyril conceives 'incarnation' in much too external a manner. There is no true unity between the Logos and the man Jesus. If the Logos becomes flesh by taking to itself a body, that body is a mere instrument, and this falls far short of what is meant by claiming that 'God was in Christ'. Cyril does indeed say that 'the Word was united with flesh animated by a living soul', but then we have to ask, 'What was this living soul, and what became of it? Was it something different from the human *hypostasis*, the personal centre of the human being, the leading edge which is set aside and replaced by the *hypostasis* of the Logos? So was it only a part of the man Jesus with which the Logos united, and certainly not the distinctively human part?'

The drift of my argument here is becoming apparent. I am suggesting that Cyril, though he does acknowledge a human soul in Jesus Christ, is repeating in a slightly different form the heresy of Apollinarius, a view which had been condemned in 381. Like Cyril, Apollinarius had a horror of any view which seemed to divide Christ into two. He sought to establish the unity by teaching that 'the Word was both the directive, intelligent principle in Jesus Christ, and also the vivifying principle of his flesh'.[6] The words translated here as 'directive, intelligent principle' seem to designate what we have been calling the *hypostasis* or 'leading edge', though the Greek word used by Apollinarius is *nous*. So there would seem to be very little difference between him and Cyril. Apollinarius annexed the 'vivifying principle' (*psyche*) as well to the Logos, whereas Cyril presumably retained a human soul. But in the Greek thought of that time, there were several different levels or grades of 'soul' (*psyche*), and the way in which both of these men talk of it suggests that what they had in mind was no more than a life principle. But both of them seem equally open to the objection that the humanity which the Logos assumed was not a complete humanity but perhaps only a framework of bones, blood, nerves and so on, serving the Logos as an instrument but having no value or significance in itself. This is again a form of docetism. The classic criticism is found in the words of Gregory of Nazianzus about the teaching of Apollinarius: 'That which [the Logos] has not assumed, he has not healed; but that which is united to his Godhead is also saved. If only half Adam fell, then that which Christ assumes and saves must be half also; but if the whole of his nature fell, it must be united to the whole nature of him that was begotten, and so be saved as a whole. Let them not therefore begrudge us our complete salvation, or clothe the Saviour only with bones and nerves and the portraiture of humanity.'[7]

One could bring further objections against the *anhypostasia* doctrine. By depriving Jesus Christ of a human hypostasis, does it not eliminate the whole historical element from his career? Perhaps there was some Platonist influence at work here, because for Plato the universal is the reality, rather than the particular. Man-in-general is more important than this or that particular man. But though it is true that Christianity claims a universal significance for Christ, it is nevertheless rooted in a concrete episode of history. It arises from a distinct person located in the stream of world history, and if that is surrendered, it becomes an ideal, again a docetic Christ quite outside the history and experience of human beings on earth.

To acknowledge that Jesus Christ was a particular human being with distinguishing characteristics – maleness, Jewishness, and all the rest – is not to deny his universal significance or to detract from his place as the representative or archetypal human being. Rather, it is a necessary condition of his universality, and does not call for such dubious notions as *anhypostasia* or man-in-general. Jesus' significance for the whole human race depends (though certainly in a very special or even unique way) on the general truth that 'no man is an island' (Donne) or an isolated individual and that each particular person is the centre of a whole nexus of relationships linking him or her to other persons and in some degree to the whole human race. This is the mystery of the solidarity of the human race, a network of connections joining our lives together in ways which are only partially understood. Such philosophers as Hegel and Whitehead have acknowledged this solidarity, but it remains largely unexplored. Paul must have had some such idea in mind when he wrote: 'Therefore as sin came into the world through one man and death through sin, and so death spread to all men because all men sinned . . . But the free gift is not like the trespass. For if many died through one man's trespass, much more have the grace of God and the free gift in the grace of that one man Jesus Christ abounded for many' (Rom. 5. 12, 15). These matters will be considered again when we come to the question 'How do we know Jesus Christ?', to be considered in Chapter 5.

A related objection is that if the directive principle in Jesus Christ was not human but divine, then to some extent his whole story becomes a sham. His resistance to temptation, his courage in the face of suffering, his obedience even to the cross, those things which evoke our deepest responses, are all the work of God in disguise. What merit was there in resisting temptation if he *could not* sin (*non posse peccare*)? What sense would there be in those inspiring words of Raymond Brown describing Jesus' progress to the cross, quoted above?[8] How could Jesus Christ be the 'representative man', not only our Redeemer but our Exemplar, if he was not really a *human* person at all?

Our investigation of the doctrine of *anhypostasia* has had mainly negative results. Yet perhaps this is not entirely the case. We have noted how the three terms, *ousia*, *physis* and *hypostasis*, were often confused. Cyril had the merit of making a clear distinction between *physis* and *hypostasis*, a distinction which is still important for theology. In the previous chapter, I mentioned only briefly the doctrine of Christ's sinlessness, and suggested that this doctrine does not pose a serious threat to accepting Christ's real humanity, for sin is not of the essence of human nature, but a corruption of it. I think we can enlarge on this somewhat, after our study of the Chalcedonian terminology. I hasten to say that a full study would demand two or three books devoted to that alone! Lampe's *Dictionary of Patristic Greek* requires no less than fourteen columns to list the various meanings and usages of *hypostasis* alone, and of course that is only the barest outline. So I hope it is not too much of an impertinence to say a little on the relation of *hypostasis* and *physis* in the light of Cyril's use of these terms.

He acknowledged two 'natures' in Christ, one human and one divine, but he held that these 'concurred' in a single 'person'. In this view of Jesus Christ, one can say very little about the divine nature, which must have been reduced to the finite level by some kind of *kenosis* or emptying. As to the human nature, we can say that it is not the same in everyone, not the same at all times and in all cultures, though possessing some common characteristics by which we recognize a human being as distinct from either an animal or an angel. This human nature is, so to speak, the raw material out of which a human person is built up. The nature consists of the desires, impulses, instincts which we all know, the driving energies of life, some deriving from bodily sources (such as hunger, thirst, sexual desire), others of a spiritual kind (desire for power and domination, desire for esteem, love for family). Our nature itself does not act, but is rather the potential for action. So I would say that

Cyril had made an advance on Leo, for the latter spoke of 'each nature in union with the other performing the acts which are proper to it'. Surely it is not the nature that performs the acts, but the person which selects and decides upon the acts proposed or made possible by the nature. So Cyril was correct in seeing that the personal centre has a kind of governing role over the nature. Actions, certainly actions which may be judged right or wrong, are performed not by the nature but by the person. This, as I suggested, is important for understanding what is meant by the sinlessness of Jesus, and in what sense he could be tempted. His complete human nature must have included the desires and instincts, both physical and spiritual, that are experienced by all human beings. These desires and instincts are neither right nor wrong, meritorious or sinful. Only when they are taken up by the personal centre do they acquire a moral status, either positive or negative. Even to feel a momentary attraction[9] is not sinful, unless it is taken up by the 'leading edge'. The attribution of sinlessness to Jesus is not something that could be empirically verified, but even in terms of the ancient terminology it is intelligible, and in no way contradicts his humanity, though it does distinguish him, perhaps in a unique way, from other men and women.

The basic fault in Cyril's christology was the very meagre place that he left for the humanity of Christ. Grillmeier remarks: 'The Alexandrian picture of Christ expressed by Cyril . . . needed constant correction. For this picture of Christ was top-heavy, since it was conceived one-sidedly, from above.'[10] It did, of course, receive some correction at the Council of Chalcedon, which met seven years after Cyril's death, and balanced the assertion that Christ is consubstantial (or 'of one being') with the Father with the compensating statement that he is of one being with us. But, as we have seen, there has been a constant drift in the church toward minimizing the humanity.

Nevertheless, in the Byzantine theology which developed in the centuries after Chalcedon, there was a new sense of the humanity of Christ, and of the significance of humanity generally, and this led to reconsiderations of the *hypostasis* of Jesus Christ and its relation to the two natures. This rethinking took place within the existing framework of ideas and was, at least to begin with, a modification of the current christology rather than a radical new departure. Perhaps it became such with the advent of Maximus the Confessor (580–662), for his approach to christology has much in common with some of the twentieth-century writers who take anthropology as their starting-point. But our concern in this chapter is confined to criticizing those elements coming from the classical christological discussions which still enjoy wide respect among some who claim to be 'orthodox', but which, because they have the appearance of minimizing or undermining the genuine humanity of Christ, are as much an offence against Chalcedonian orthodoxy as are views which diminish or deny Christ's divinity.

We have already given considerable attention to the doctrine of *anhypostasia* and have, I believe, found it wanting. Already in the sixth century some theologians were modifying the doctrine, and it was being transformed into the view called *enhypostasia*, though this noun formation, like *anhypostasia*, was invented by theologians long after the idea which it designates had been conceived and discussed. I gave a brief explanation of the idea at the beginning of the chapter,[11] but I must now go into more detail.

One of the most careful explanations of *enhypostasia* and one which brings out clearly its high valuation of humanity is found in the British theologian H. M. Relton, who revived the concept in his own important work, *A Study in Christology*, published in 1917. His presuppositions were much like my own. He believed that 'the truly human character of the Word made flesh' had been obscured in the development of christology, and he believed too that 'there is an essential affinity between the human and the divine', and that this is a necessary condition for the possibility of incarnation. The heart of his argument is that:

> The presupposition of the doctrine of *enhypostasia* is the existence of such an affinity between the human and the divine as to make the advent of the latter into the former not the advent of some alien element, but the advent of something which by its very constitution and nature could coalesce with the human, and by its union with and subsistence in the human, give to the latter a completeness and perfection which it could receive in no other way.[12]

This is a statement of the *enhypostasia* doctrine by a twentieth-century theologian, and it is phrased in language which most people in the modern age can understand. I think, however, he is saying very much what certain theologians of the sixth century were saying, though it is difficult for the modern reader to enter into the thought of these Byzantine theologians. According to Grillmeier, their view was that 'with the incarnation of the Word, a new species has entered into the hierarchy of beings'.[13] A distant parallel from modern times might be some of the events that occurred in Russia after the Revolution of 1917. Lenin was regarded as the saviour of the people, even as the greatest genius in history. When he died in 1924, his brain was handed over to scientists so that they might study what made him so unique. His virtues were destined to be extended to the whole nation, perhaps even to all mankind, and a philosopher of those days invented the expression *Homo sovieticus*, to designate the new species that had appeared and to differentiate it from such lesser breeds as *Homo sapiens* and *Homo neanderthalensis*. Among the sixth-century theologians who (without actually using the word *enhypostasia*) taught that the person (*hypostasis*) of Jesus Christ was a unique divine-human entity, constituted by the *hypostasis* of the Logos containing in itself the *hypostasis* of the man Jesus, there was likewise the belief that a new species had appeared. So we find expressions like the following: 'Through the mystery of the incarnation, there is created a new being (*ousia*) of absolute singularity, a new species in the hierarchy of beings' (Sergius Scholasticus); 'The *hypostasis*, the concrete person Jesus Christ, is neither simply divine nor simply human, but a *tertium quid*' (Leontius of Byzantium). This Leontius is the name that has become chiefly associated with *enhypostasia*, but he was for a long time confused with his contemporary, Leontius of Jerusalem.[14]

We may think that *enhypostasia* is a marked advance on *anhypostasia*, and we may think too that the idea of a *hypostasis* that is 'neither simply human nor simply divine' is a better solution than Cyril's denial that there is a human *hypostasis* in Christ and better than the one-sided idea that the human *hypostasis* is included within the *hypostasis* of the Logos. One could also claim that it fits very well with the words of the Chalcedonian Definition: 'one and the same Christ, Son, Lord, Only-begotten, recognized in two natures, without confusion, without change, without division, without separation; the distinction of natures being in no way annulled by the union, but rather the characteristics of each nature being preserved and coming together to form one person and subsistence, not as parted or separated into two persons, but one and the same Son and only-begotten God the Word, Lord Jesus Christ.' *Enhypostasia* seems to meet these requirements, especially if we say that the *hypostasis* which is neither simply divine nor simply human embraces both the divine and the human, rather than saying that the human element is taken into the divine *hypostasis*.

But we should be aware that *enhypostasis* may be creating as many problems as it is supposed to solve. For does it not indeed make Christ a new species, and therefore just as effectively separate him from the rest of the human race as Cyril (and Apollinarius) did, and therefore make him irrelevant to the spiritual quest of the human race? We seem to be caught up again in the dilemma which Schleiermacher described – we must neither obliterate the distinction between Christ and other men and women, nor exaggerate it to the point where it becomes separation. This last point could be put in a slightly different way: we must understand the difference between Christ and the rest of humanity as one of degree, rather than of kind. If this sounds somewhat shocking to a Christian believer, let me add that a difference of degree may be so great that for all practical purposes it counts as a difference of kind. Christ is still different, he still has a unique relation to the Father, he is still the divine Christ, the Mediator between God and the human race. But he is not an anomaly in the universe, but rather, as we shall see later, the clue both to its origin and its destiny. The eternal Word expresses itself in everything, because indeed it is the archetype of everything, but above all in Jesus Christ. He is the God-man, and his closeness to God, indeed, his unity with God, does not annul his true humanity.

In criticizing these two ancient doctrines of *anhypostasia* and *enhypostasia*, I have tried not to be unmindful of the fact that they were stages, perhaps necessary stages, on the way towards a deeper understanding of Jesus Christ, and that the authors of these ideas were questers like ourselves, and did not hesitate to acknowledge that the mysteries both of God and of his creation are always greater than our minds can encompass. But in the case of the two traditional ideas we have been examining, I think that theological speculation has got out of hand and may even have lost touch with reality. At least, they have removed Jesus Christ from human reality and made him into an anomaly. Confronted with such notions, we have to bear in mind a truth that was succinctly stated by John Meyendorff: 'Human nature at the contact of God does not disappear; on the contrary, it becomes fully human.'[15]

4

A Critique of Adoptionism

In the first three chapters of this book, I have been stressing the need in christology for a more adequate recognition of the full humanity of Jesus Christ, since I believe that both in theology and in popular piety his truly human nature has been obscured, even to the point of an unconscious docetism. But when someone tries to correct this long-standing bias, he or she may easily overshoot the mark and deprive Jesus of his distinctiveness – that 'something more', as I have been calling it, which Christian believers have expressed in a doctrine of incarnation. Yet when the doctrine of incarnation (or some equivalent doctrine) is removed, then, although the Christian faith may become more acceptable to certain minds, it has also been made so bland that it could hardly be called a 'gospel' any more. The paradox of the God-man is hard to believe, but Christianity without the paradox loses much of its significance. I have made it clear that we can scarcely hope to resolve that para-dox, but we do have to make room for both sides of it. So if we have so far been concerned chiefly to defend the true humanity of Jesus Christ, his 'consubstantiality' with us, it is time to begin redressing the balance and to consider what makes him distinct from ordinary men and women, what makes him, in the traditional language, 'consubstantial' with God the Father.

As a first step toward such redressment, we shall engage in a critique of adoptionism, the type of christological theory which, it is usually believed, so emphasizes the humanity of Christ that it rules out any special ontological or metaphysical relation between him and the Father. When one speaks of adoptionism, one is, of course, using a metaphor. In traditional Christian language, Jesus Christ is often said to be 'begotten' of God the Father. This is obviously figurative language, but the point of it is that Jesus Christ does somehow share in the being or substance of God, and this relation is not an external one or a temporary one, but belongs to the inmost being of Jesus, and is comparable to the relation between a child and his or her natural father. When one speaks of 'adoption', the relation between father and child is not one of 'being' or 'substance', though it may be as much a relation of love as would be the case in a 'blood' relationship or even more so. It is clear that difficult questions arise. How important is it to insist on a special ontological relation of Jesus Christ to the Father? How different must his relationship be from yours and mine to safeguard his position as Redeemer and Lord, yet without separating him from the human condition and making him something other than a member of the human race? These questions and others will have to be faced, but it is worth mentioning them now if only to make it clear that adoptionism is not just some frightful heresy, but in some cases at least, an honest attempt to grapple with the baffling paradox of the God-man. A critique must not only criticize weaknesses but recognize and build on strengths when they are found.

But before we get into these difficult questions, a little needs to be said about the term 'adoptionism', and the historical background. Like many other technical theological terms, such as *anhypostasia*, discussed in Chapter 3, the word 'adoptionism' came into use long after the views which it represents had appeared in the church's thinking about Jesus Christ. There are at least three contexts in which the term 'adoptionism' is used by modern critics. 1. There was a primitive adoptionism which appeared very early in Christian history. To begin with, it was a perfectly acceptable way of speaking about Jesus Christ, but by the third century it had hardened into a definite theory, which was adjudged to be heretical. Whether it deserved to be so adjudged is a question to which we shall have to return. 2. There were in Spain in the eighth century some very specific theological speculations called 'adoptianism' (note the spelling), and these also were considered heretical, but nowadays they have only an antiquarian interest. 3. Finally, the adoptionist label has been bandied around pretty freely in modern times as an imprecise term of abuse, directed against theologians who in one way or another have questioned in general or in details some of the christological dogmas formuated by the early councils, and intended to safeguard the distinctive status of Jesus Christ.

1. Something like a primitive adoptionism has been claimed by some scholars to be present in the New Testament. John Knox, for instance, says:

The question is not whether the author of Luke-Acts held an adoptionist christology, but whether evidence for the primitive existence of such a christology is to be found in his work. I do not see how we can escape the conclusion that it is. To cite the clearest example, 'God has made this Jesus whom you crucified both Lord and Christ' (Acts 2. 36). How can this be interpreted to mean anything else than that the man Jesus, crucified simply as

such, was at the resurrection exalted to his present
messianic status?[1]

Knox believed therefore that the primitive christology
was adoptionist, in the sense that Jesus was a man approved
by God and elected by God to be the Christ, an election
confirmed and declared by the resurrection. Yet Knox also
believed that this christology did not last for long. In the
same sermon in which Peter had spoken of Jesus being
'made' both Lord and Christ, he had also said that these
things had happened 'according to the definite plan and
foreknowledge of God' (Acts 2. 23). So Knox claims that an
'affirmation of pre-existence was implicit in the story from
the beginning . . . It would have been impossible for any
Jewish Christian to entertain even for a little while the
notion that God had merely happened to find a man worthy
of becoming the Messiah.'[2] Knox believed that it was only a
short step from the belief that Jesus had 'pre-existed' in
the mind and purpose of God to the conception of a pre-
existing hypostasis or personal pre-existence, such as is
found in later Christian belief. I myself am inclined to think
that we may equate pre-existence in the mind of God with
real pre-existence, and that we do not need to carry speculation on this point any further. At any rate, it would seem
that even in the very earliest days of Christianity, when
theology was only beginning to stir, so to speak, it was felt
that a simple adoptionism was somehow inadequate and
that there had to be some pre-existent ground, however, it
might be defined.

It is often thought that we find a much more elaborate
christology in Paul, but it is doubtful if Paul is saying anything essentially different from the preaching of Peter. I
have mentioned Peter first, because his sermon is said to

have been given at the very birth of the church, on the Feast of Pentecost. We have to remember, however, that Luke's report of the sermon comes from several decades later. Some of Paul's letters, on the other hand, may be only twenty years later than Pentecost, and constitute our earliest *written* evidence for the christological beliefs of the earliest Christians. I accept that the main strand in Paul's christology could be described as adoptionist, though he too recognizes that a simple adoptionism is inadequate and, like the Peter of Acts, adds further thoughts about the provenance of Christ. The opening verses of the letter to the Romans have a strong adoptionist flavour, for they speak of 'the gospel concerning [God's] Son, who was descended from David according to the flesh, and designated Son of God in power according to the Spirit of holiness by his resurrection from the dead' (Rom. 1. 3–4). A natural reading of these verses would suggest that Jesus was a fully human being descended from David (there is no mention of a virginal conception) who after the resurrection is designated Son of God. What is meant here by 'designated' (the RSV translation of *horisthentos*)? Does it simply mean that the resurrection 'declared' or 'made public' an already existing state of affairs? Perhaps we could accept this if we pay attention to other letters of Paul. But if we took it to mean that the resurrection brought into being Jesus' status as Son of God, this would be a much more adoptionist reading.

However, Paul has a much fuller christology than what we can find in the beginning of Romans. It is based on a comparison and contrast of the figures of Adam and Jesus. We find it in the fifth chapter of Romans and, in a different form, in I Corinthians. It is a christology 'from below', that is to say, based on the humanity of Christ, but it is not adoptionist and shows that a christology which begins from the human Christ need not be adoptionist. Two human beings (*anthropoi*) are set over against one another. Through one of them (Adam) sin and death have entered the world, and have spread through all members of the human race. Through the other (Jesus Christ) has come righteousness, and this too has spread out to many through justifying grace. Just as sin brings death, so righteousness brings life. In fact, we could say that a new humanity appears with Christ, a humanity orientated on righteousness and life. Adam is a mythological figure, Jesus an historical one, but they are both human. The fact that one is mythical, the other historical, is not important for Paul. He considers them both as human beings. Adam represents the 'average man' in the sense that his experience is the experience of all the other human beings who have followed him on this planet. If it was God's intention that the human being should bear his image and likeness in the created realm, then we would have to say that Adam is a failed human being, and the 'average man or woman' is no more than an approximation to a human being. Jesus Christ is the representative human being in a different sense: not an example of the average specimen, but the 'true man', the realization of the divine purpose for man. Because he is the true man, he also brings to realization the image and likeness of God on the finite level. In Paul's words, 'He is the image of the invisible God' (Col. 1. 15). Paul lays too much stress on the concept of grace for us to suppose that, to adapt the words of John Knox, there 'happens' to be a human being who fulfils the potentiality of his humanity, but it is doubtful whether Paul invokes a doctrine of pre-existence to break out of a humanistic interpretation of christhood.

But, it may be asked, what about the famous Christ hymn

in Philippians, whether it was actually composed by Paul or is quoted by him from some pre-Pauline source? As I have argued elsewhere,[3] it seems to me that James Dunn has provided a persuasive exegesis of this hymn without having to impute a doctrine of pre-existence to Paul, even in the use of the words, 'though he was in the form of God, [he] did not count equality with God a thing to be grasped, but emptied himself, taking the form of a servant, being born in the likeness of men' (Phil. 2. 6–7). So I do not think the adoptionist mould can be broken only by the introduction of a doctrine of pre-existence. Paul does break it by his broad declaration, 'If anyone is in Christ, he is a new creation; the old has passed away, behold, the new has come. All this is from God' (II Cor. 5. 17–18).

What, in any case, would be required by a doctrine of pre-existence? We might be quite willing to accept that, even on the basis of a natural theology, we could agree that in the infinite riches of the divine Being it is necessary to distinguish God as he is in himself, far transcending our human knowledge, and God as he turns towards, and reveals himself in, his creation; or, in trinitarian language, between God the Father and God the Logos. Then one could certainly affirm that God the Logos is co-eternal with God the Father, and so if the Word became flesh in Jesus, the Word pre-existed the appearance on earth of Jesus Christ. But does this amount to a pre-existence of Jesus Christ? We have seen reason above to reject the identification of the person or *hypostasis* of Jesus with the *hypostasis* of the Logos (Apollinarianism and allied views).[4] If the incarnation, the true union of the outgoing Logos of God with the man Jesus of Nazareth, is a reality and not just appearance, then the *hypostasis* of Jesus the Christ is something new, not identical with the hypostasis of the hitherto discarnate Logos. The body surely has a share in the constitution of a person.

I suppose that in a very broad sense it could be said that the body of Jesus or anyone's body was pre-existent, in so far as it must be made out of particles that have existed for ages in the physical world. Incarnation can be viewed as a process that began with creation and has gone on through many stages, as indeed Teilhard de Chardin has depicted it in his vision of a cosmos in evolution. But this is different from the idea of a personal pre-existence of Jesus Christ, and is nearer to the idea of a pre-existence in the mind and purpose of God, which, as was suggested above, may be a perfectly adequate way of conceiving Christ's pre-existence.

I think therefore that the statement that the earliest christology, such as we find it in early sermons in Acts or in the epistles of Paul, was adoptionist can be made only if it is heavily qualified. It must have been felt from the first to be inadequate, and, as Knox agrees, it did not last for long. It was modified either by the assertion that the career of Jesus had been foreordained by God, or by the further idea that in some way Jesus Christ had pre-existed. It is quite likely, however, that a full-blown belief in pre-existence came only with the latest of the New Testament writings, in particular the Gospel of John.

Certainly, adoptionism was one strand in the earliest christologies, but it never stood simply by itself. Since adoptionism stresses the humanity of Jesus Christ, it is not surprising that it would have been influential in the earliest period, when the memory of the human Jesus was still fresh. To quote Knox again, 'It would not have occurred to anyone [at that time] to affirm that Jesus was human, for the obvious reason that it would not have occurred to anyone that he might have been anything else.'[5] Yet I say that adoptionism never stood by itself, and virtually from the beginning was felt to be inadequate. Those who had come in touch with Jesus had recognized in him something distinctive, something 'more', as I have been calling it. Through him, they had had salvific experiences of one kind or another – a new sense of God, or of meaning in their own lives, of spiritual renewal, or whatever it may have been, and this they tried to express in their language about Christ. They felt that just to recognize him as a true man of God or as a new prophet, perhaps even the greatest, or the Messiah himself – they felt that somehow this did not go far enough. New ways of speaking had to be found, and the first steps were being taken toward the development of what in the next few centuries would emerge as the orthodox christology.

We must be aware, of course, that when modern scholars speak of adoptionism in the New Testament, their language is anachronistic. Strictly speaking, adoptionism only emerges when there is an alternative 'orthodox' view with which to contrast it. In the early Christian period, there were various groups of Jewish Christians, usually called Ebionites, who probably did hold beliefs that were simply adoptionist, but they could hardly be considered heretical unless they held their beliefs in conscious opposition to the church's teaching. Perhaps in the whole of the pre-Nicene period, while there was still a certain measure of fluidity in doctrine, people who thought of Jesus as no more than a man approved by God should not be accused of transgressing an orthodoxy which had not yet fully emerged.

Perhaps we should even be willing to extend the same tolerance to the man who became the most famous or notorious of all adoptionists, Paul of Samosata, Bishop of Antioch about sixty years before the Council of Nicaea.

According to Eusebius, this Paul was a worldly man who had a luxurious life-style and enjoyed the adulation of the public.[6] This unbecoming behaviour in a bishop may have done more harm to Paul's reputation than his theological opinions, which are hard to pin down and may not have been so unorthodox as they were later judged to be. But though it has become fashionable nowadays to attempt the rehabilitation of heretics, this might not prove easy in the case of Paul of Samosata.

Paul was probably the first to introduce the language of 'from above' and 'from below' into christological discourse. He is reported to have said, 'The Word is from above, Jesus Christ is a man from below (literally, "from here").' In the Greek, this sentence reads: '*Logos men anothen, Iesous de Christos anthropos enteuthen.*' There might seem to be little wrong with this sentence, but there is considerable doubt as to how the Word and the human Jesus were understood to be related. According to his critics, the relation was one of 'friendship' rather than of 'substance' or 'being', though I think it could be argued that a relationship of love is an ontological relationship, founded in the being of those participating in it. However, there is further doubt about how Paul understood the relation of the Logos to God the Father, whom he seems to have conceived in a strictly unitarian or monolithic manner. In any case, Paul's colleagues in the episcopate were not persuaded that his views were acceptable, and condemned them in synod.

Let me sum up what we have learned in this brief survey of 'primitive' adoptionism. It did have the merit of emphasizing the humanity of Christ, and later I shall return to this point. But it seemed to suggest that Jesus Christ was no more than a product of human history, and the conclusion might well be that humanity of itself can rise toward God in spite of the sin in our history. Yet such a view does not come to expression even in Paul of Samosata, who seeks to combine the 'coming down' of the Logos with the human origin of Jesus 'from here'. In the biblical passages having an adoptionist tendency, there is no tendency to isolate it from a fuller christology that would acknowledge that 'all this is from God', and that the Logos 'assumes' a human life rather than that a human being rises to the level of the divine.

2. We can quickly pass over the second brand of adoptionism, for, as was said near the beginning of the chapter, it has nowadays no more than an antiquarian interest. It was a heretical movement in Spain during the eighth century. Those who maintained it separated the divine Word from the human Jesus so sharply that they claimed that the latter could be only the 'adoptive' Son of God, not a true Son. Presumably, though, one might say that however the 'Son of God' is defined, the expression is, from a human point of view, inescapably figurative.

3. We pass on now to the question of adoptionism in modern theology. I remarked at the beginning of the chapter that the term 'adoptionism' seems nowadays to be an ill-defined term of abuse reserved for theologians who begin their christological reflections from the humanity of Jesus or who more generally are determined to give to that humanity its full place. So we find Emil Brunner writing, 'Paul of Samosata might be described as the first Ritschlian, or in a more general way as the first modern theologian.'[7] This may be interpreted as a put-down of Paul of Samosata or of modern theology or of both. This recent and contemporary use of the term 'adoptionism' is too vague and too broadly applied to be easily defined. When in 1977 I was reviewing the volume of essays entitled *The Myth of God*

Incarnate, I suggested three criteria that might be used to distinguish between an incarnational christology and christologies of a reductionist kind. These criteria were: (a) The initiative is from God, not man. (b) God is deeply involved in his creation. (c) The centre of this initiative and involvement is Jesus Christ.[8] One would have to apply these criteria to individual cases, rather than make an adverse judgement on 'modern theology' in general. So I would not be able to agree with Eric Mascall's sweeping condemnation of 'the modern neo-adoptionism of which Knox, Pittenger and Robinson are in their various ways exponents'.[9]

Let us consider briefly each of the three theologians about whom Mascall complained. Of John Knox, we have said quite a lot already. It is true, as we have seen, that he could speak of an 'original adoptionism'[10] in Peter's Pentecost sermon, but he tells us at once that this was only a momentary phase, and was (apparently simultaneously) corrected by Peter's statement that behind Jesus was the predestining act of God the Father. It is true also that Knox writes, 'I believe it can be said not only that the most primitive christology – what we have been calling "adoptionism" – is the minimally essential christology, but also that in its basic structure it was, and might conceivably have continued to be, an entirely adequate christology.'[11] I find it hard to believe that this really represents Knox's view, having regard both to what he had said earlier about the primitive christology's having survived for a very short time, and what he says later (all these views are expressed in the same book) to the effect that 'the old pattern' (adoptionism) became inadequate and 'by a kind of necessity' yielded to a new pattern which included the idea of pre-existence. To show that Knox was at least open to the idea of a christology going beyond a bare adoptionism, one might also point to the fact that following on his statement about the possibility that adoptionism might have become the permanent christology of the church, he has a footnote containing a long quotation from Rahner. Part of the quotation reads:

> Let us take so central an assertion of the Scriptures as the statement that Jesus is the Messiah and as such has become Lord in the course of his life, death and resurrection. Is it agreed that this assertion has simply been made obsolete by the doctrine of the metaphysical Sonship, as *we* recognize it and express it in the Chalcedonian definition, and that its only real interest for us now is historical? Is the christology of the Acts of the Apostles, which begins from below, with the human experience of Jesus, merely primitive? Or has it something special to say to us, which classical christology does not say with the same clarity?[12]

I am not, of course, trying to assimilate Knox's teaching to that of Rahner (to whom I shall shortly return), but simply trying to show that one should not be too hasty in dismissing as 'adoptionism' views which insist on the true humanity of Jesus Christ, and a process of development both in the church's understanding of him and in his own self-understanding.

When we turn to Norman Pittenger, the second of the three Anglican theologians indicted by Dr Mascall, we find the following criticism: 'Dr W. N. Pittenger, in his books *The Word Incarnate* and *Christology Reconsidered*, expounds what to everyone but himself is plainly an adoptionist doctrine, though he has persuaded himself that it is what

Chalcedon was really trying to say. The impression that he leaves is not that he was deliberately championing Nestorianism against Chalcedonianism but that he was somehow incapable of seeing the difference between the two positions.'[13] That was not the impression which Pittenger's book left with me, and the judgment strikes me as unfair. We find him saying, 'Thus we can see that to all eternity the whole issue of Christianity is found in the problems which the early Church faced, and if the intention which determined the classical formulations adopted at that time (although not necessarily the words) be denied, Christianity is certainly destroyed.'[14] These do not sound like the sentiments of someone who is championing Nestorianism against Chalcedonianism! But Pittenger was determined to maintain the full humanity of Jesus Christ, and in this was thoroughly Chalcedonian. It is true that more than once in his writings, he declares that the difference between Jesus Christ and other human beings is one of degree, rather than of kind, but in saying this I think he is simply claiming that the distinctiveness of Christ is conceivable within the category of humanity, and does not demand the separation of Christ from mankind into another species. That would surely be a denial of incarnation. In any case, a difference in degree may be so important that it makes 'all the difference', as we say. Pittenger, as a process theologian, seeks continuities rather than sudden leaps. For him (and I agree) Jesus Christ is not an anomaly in the universe but rather the summing up in a single point, the 'focus', of the divine Logos that is present and active in the whole creation.

The third theologian mentioned among the 'neo-adoptionists' was John A. T. Robinson, whose major contribution to christology was the book entitled *The Human Face of God*. Again I am not persuaded that the adoptionist label was deserved. When the collection of essays, *The Myth of God Incarnate*, was published in 1977, Robinson reviewed it very severely, and upheld the idea of incarnation, though not necessarily in the language that has sometimes been used. But once again, a theologian deserves to be judged by his intentions, and Robinson tells us that his intention was to affirm all that the New Testament and the tradition derived from it had claimed for Jesus Christ. He wrote: 'I am wishing to affirm Jesus as the Son of God as the New Testament speaks of him, as the one who was called at his baptism and vindicated at his resurrection to *be* God's decisive word to men, the embodiment of his nature and the enactment of his will.'[15] I do not think that this view can properly be called adoptionist, even having regard to the imprecise usages of that word.

Here I find myself once again mentioning the imprecision of the word 'adoptionist'. There is a metaphorical element in the expression, but it is not clear just how apposite this figure of speech is. Perhaps it would be helpful first of all to call to mind the words of the so-called Athanasian Creed, which, I think, give a remarkably clear statement of the orthodox Christian teaching concerning the incarnation. The Creed declares:

Furthermore, it is necessary to everlasting salvation that one also believe rightly the incarnation of our Lord Jesus Christ.

For the right faith is, that we believe and confess, that our Lord Jesus Christ, the son of God, is God and man;

God, of the substance of the Father, begotten before the worlds, and man, of the substance of his Mother, born in the world;

Complete God and complete man, of a reasonable soul
and human flesh subsisting;
Equal to the Father as touching his Godhead; and
inferior to the Father as touching his manhood.
Who, although he be God and man, yet he is not two, but
one Christ;
One, not by conversion of the Godhead into flesh, but by
taking of the manhood into God;
One altogether, not by confusion of substance, but by
unity of person.
For as the reasonable soul and flesh is one man, so God
and man is one Christ.

Let me just take from this a few points that will help to
clarify this discussion of adoptionism. Jesus Christ is, in
agreement with Chalcedon, said to share completely in the
divine being and in human being, but the further point is
made that he is equal to the Father in respect of his deity,
inferior in respect of his humanity. What does this mean? It
seems to me to be taking into account the limitations that
would necessarily be present in any incarnation. God is
infinite, the human being is finite, so God cannot be con-
tained in a human life. In any incarnation, God must be, so
to speak, 'dimmed down'. There are perhaps properties of
God, most importantly, love, which is more than a property
for it is the very being of God – 'God *is* love' (1 John 4. 8),
and these properties can be present in a human life. There
are other properties, such as omnipotence and omniscience,
which imply the infinitude of God, and, as the kenoticists
recognized, cannot be present in a human life. So if we
speak of an incarnation, this cannot mean a simple identity
of God with Christ, and indeed I do not think that this has
ever been the true Christian teaching. It is the Word, the

Logos, the Second Person of the Trinity that is present in Christ; and even the Logos continued to fill the world and was not confined to Jesus Christ.[16]

If we now return to the Athanasian Creed, I think we shall find confirmation of the points I have just been making. There we read that Jesus Christ is 'One, not by conversion of the Godhead into flesh, but by taking of the manhood into God; One altogether, not by confusion of substance, but by unity of person'. 'The Word was made flesh' cannot mean that God was transformed into a finite being, so 'conversion of the Godhead into flesh' is ruled out. Instead of that, we are told, there is a 'taking' or 'assuming' of humanity into God. The human being is (as far as our knowledge goes) the only finite being made in the image and likeness of God, and so the only finite being that could be the locus of an incarnation. Jesus Christ was said by Schleiermacher to be 'the completion of the creation of man',[17] the only true man who fulfils the Creator's intention, and is 'the image (*eikon*) of the invisible God' (Col. 1. 15). So the divinity of Jesus Christ is to be seen in his perfected humanity. John Knox, towards the end of that book in which we have noted various stages in his thinking about Jesus Christ, claimed that 'the divine Lord is none other than the human Jesus exalted – his divinity thus being a transformed, a redeemed and redemptive humanity'.[18] There is nothing reductionist in this statement. Adoptionism, whether it is rightly or wrongly so-called, need not in any way impugn the unique status of Jesus Christ and would only do so if it refused to develop beyond a minimalist stage in christological reflection. But it makes its own important affirmative contribution in compelling us to recognize the importance of the humanity in the constitution of the God-man. 'Only someone who forgets that the essence of man is to be unbounded,' writes Rahner, 'can suppose that it is impossible for there to be a man, who, precisely by being man in the fullest sense (which we never attain) is God's existence into the world.'[19]

The assertions of Knox and Rahner just quoted – that 'the divinity of Christ is a transformed, a redeemed and redemptive humanity' (Knox), or that 'Christ is a man, who, precisely by being man in the fullest sense . . . is God's existence into the world' (Rahner) may seem to us at first sight to be quite opposed to the orthodox teaching of the church on the person of Jesus Christ. Do they not altogether blur the absolute distinction that there must be between God the Creator and his human creatures? Do they not reduce Jesus Christ entirely to the human level? Certainly the views of the two-theologians mentioned are radical, but if we ponder them carefully, I think that we may find that they are not opposed to either the spirit or even the language of the traditional teachings.

What do we mean when we say that there is an 'absolute' difference between God and man? Some theologians who have emphasized the divine transcendence have spoken of God as the 'wholly other', and clearly there is in God a depth of being far beyond anything that the human mind can conceive. In that sense, there is a difference that may be called 'absolute'. But there must also be some affinity between God and man, otherwise it is hard to see how human beings could ever have come to believe in the reality of a God, or how anything like an incarnation could have come about. We can say, with Karl Barth, that there is a 'humanity' in God, in the sense that God in his creativity conceived a being who, on the finite level, might express his own 'image and likeness'. This would imply also that the human being would have the capacity of receiving progressively the Spirit of God and so growing more perfectly into the image and likeness of God. This, however, would happen without transgressing the bounds of finite humanity. It would be a process which the church fathers did not hesitate to call *theopoiesis* or 'deification'. This did not mean that the human being became God or a part of God, but that he or she became an image or icon of those qualities of deity that can be manifested on the finite level. The person's humanity is not abolished, but it is transfigured and brought to its highest potential. This, I believe, is a fair interpretation of how Knox and Rahner and others understand 'incarnation'.

When I quoted earlier in the chapter a part of the Athanasian Creed, I drew attention especially to the clauses which say of Christ that 'although he be God and man, yet he is not two but one Christ; One, not by conversion of the Godhood into flesh, but by taking of the manhood into God; One altogether, not by confusion of substance, but by unity of person'. I would claim that the interpretation of incarnation just given is in conformity with this ancient credal statement, and further, as I have been arguing in several contexts, that the unitary person, leading edge, or *hypostasis* of Jesus was not the *hypostasis* of the divine Logos displacing the human *hypostasis* and using the body of Jesus as a mere instrument, nor was it a composite *hypostasis* constituting Jesus a new species distinct from *homo sapiens*, but was the human *hypostasis* transfigured by a constant immersion in the divine Spirit. But I think that our human theology has its limitations, and that one could go on for ever refining and arguing about the subtle concepts that have been used in christological debates.

Finally, perhaps, in this as in some other theological questions, we have to acknowlege that our concepts are inadequate, and fall back on images which can often give us a clearer understanding. There is one image that has long appealed to me. It occurs in several of the Fathers, from Origen to John of Damascus. It offers the picture of a mass of iron being placed in a fire and constantly receiving the heat of the fire, so that it is fully permeated and transmits the light and heat it is receiving from the source. The iron does not cease to be iron, it has not been mixed with another metal, for fire is a different kind of being, yet the iron has become something more. So Christ has a complete human nature, but is 'something more' through his steady immersion in God.

5

How Do We Know Jesus Christ?

At the beginning of Chapter 2, I mentioned that virtually no one who has studied the question in any serious way doubts that there really existed a person called Jesus of Nazareth in the first century of our era. It was this Jesus who soon after his death (and perhaps even in his lifetime) was recognized as the Christ or Messiah, the anointed one who was expected by many devout Jews to come and deliver them from their troubles. So he became known by the fuller expression 'Jesus Christ', an expression which combines his personal name, Jesus, with the title, Christ, though with the rise of Christianity outside its original home in Palestine, the title Christ tended to become simply a part of the name Jesus Christ. How then do we know him? – and in asking that question, we are implying that we think it worthwhile to know this person, even though he lived two millennia before us in a very different culture.

In earlier chapters, I have gone out of my way to emphasize the genuine humanity of Jesus Christ, since I think it has often been neglected. But even so, I have several times insisted that there was something 'more' to Jesus, something which I admitted is very hard to define, though we might believe it is the inner or ultimate reality of Jesus, his christhood, those qualities in virtue of which the historical Jesus of Nazareth was recognized as the Christ of faith. It was what Paul meant when he said in apparently simple language, 'God was in Christ' (II Cor. 5. 19) and what the Chalcedonian fathers said in more complicated language when they taught that in the person of Jesus Christ there concur two natures, a human and a divine. But how do we know this person? What is our warrant for making such claims concerning him?

I think that first of all, we have to ask what we mean by 'knowing'. Not all knowledge is alike, and we have to be clear what kind of knowing we are talking about. The fact that there are contrasting ways of knowing has been recognized by many philosophers of different persuasions. Bertrand Russell wrote an essay with the title, 'Knowledge by Acquaintance and Knowledge by Description', in which he discusses from a strictly epistemological viewpoint the kind of knowledge that we have of, for example, sense-data, colours and sounds, a direct knowledge which differs from the knowledge that we have of, let us say, the Battle of the Somme, a knowledge derived from history-books and other reports.[1] Closer to our own concern with christology is Martin Buber's famous book, *I and Thou*, distinguishing a knowledge involving the whole person from a more detached or observational kind of knowing. Attempts have been made also to distinguish between knowledge by participation, where there is some kind of unity between the knower and what is known, and the knowledge in which the knower stands outside or over against what is known. I think that in modern times it is, in each of the cases I have mentioned, the second kind of knowledge that has come to be more highly prized – indeed, some would claim that only objective knowledge, the knowledge that such and such is the case, deserves to be called 'knowledge'. But that is an absurd narrowing of what we mean by knowing. Let us suppose someone has applied for an academic post. He will have sent a letter telling where he went to school, what college or university he attended, what qualifications he acquired, what his teaching experience has been and so on. The committee making the appointment will learn quite a lot from the letter and from any supporting references, but they will almost certainly ask for an interview as well, when they can directly confront and converse with the candidate and at least go some way towards knowing him directly.

In the case of Jesus Christ, there are some basic testimonies which come from the past and which tell us quite a lot about him. People sometimes complain that our knowledge from such sources is slight, but it is surely enough to yield a fairly clear picture. From the four Gospels, the rest of the New Testament, a few scattered references in pagan literature, and from the labours of historians who for several centuries have been sifting this material and subjecting it to scrutiny, we can build up a picture of Jesus, and supplement it to some extent from what we learn from other sources about the social and political conditions prevailing at that time. I say this objective kind of knowing has a priority in our time. This fact explains the importance of the 'quest for the historical Jesus' in the nineteenth century, which is still pursued today. There was a desire to cut out all the theological accretions and get down to the facts of the human being Jesus of Nazareth. Undoubtedly there was a reductionist motive in all this. It wanted to eliminate what I have, with deliberate vagueness, called the 'more' in Jesus Christ in order to lay bare the simple humanity of a man whom a superstitious age (as they judged it to be) had exalted to supernatural rank.

Of course, that result never was achieved. I am certainly not taking a negative attitude toward historical research into the career of Jesus. I think we can learn much from it, not least that Jesus is not just an imaginary figure constructed out of the religious yearnings of Jewish visionaries but a definite and even disconcerting fact of world history. But do we know Jesus only through the testimony of the past? Even if our sources were more copious so that we had something like a complete biography of Jesus rather than a sketch of, at most, the last three years of his life, would that in itself bring us to an understanding of the 'more'? Would it show that Jesus is indeed the Christ, or the Son of God or whatever expression may be used to express what is so special in Jesus, what has demanded for him the unique place that he has in Christian faith? Would we not, like the members of our academic committee, have to follow up our reading of the biographical notes with something like an interview, though an interview in which we might find ourselves to be the interviewees, not the interviewers?

What, then? Am I suggesting that there can be not only knowledge *about* Jesus, but a *direct* knowledge, a knowledge by acquaintance? And is that not absurd, considering that Jesus died all those centuries ago? He did indeed die, probably in 33 CE, but his followers believe that in some sense he lives on after his death as the risen Christ. I do not propose to discuss the meaning of resurrection at this point, though I shall come back to it in my final chapter. But leaving aside for the time being what is meant by 'resurrection', no one can deny that the influence of Jesus Christ after his death was incomparably greater than it had been while he was still alive in his Palestinian ministry and that his disciples through the ages have claimed not only to know the recorded events of Christ's career, including his resurrection, but to know Christ himself in various ways. I want now to consider some of the claims of Christians to have had a direct knowledge of Christ in the centuries that have passed since he lived in our earthly history.

The first point to be made is that we should not distinguish too sharply between the knowledge that we have from the testimony of the past and the knowledge that we have in present experience. Although the knowledge that comes to us from the New Testament is mediated knowledge, passed on to us by the evangelists, and presumably passed on to them, probably in oral form, by still earlier Christian disciples, we can experience through the language even today something of the power of that person whom we call Jesus Christ. We hear his words, for instance, in the Sermon on the Mount, and many Christians have heard them – and perhaps all Christians should have heard them – as if they were hearing the voice of Jesus himself. That is why some men and women who eventually became leaders and saints in the church have testified that in listening to a Gospel reading or a sermon, Christ's words spoke directly to them and this led them to change their whole manner of life and to undertake some difficult Christian work. If this is true of the reading and preaching of the New Testament, it is even more true of the sacraments, especially the eucharist. Christians speak of a 'real presence' of Christ in this sacrament, and his words, 'Do this for the recalling of me!' (Luke 22. 19; I Cor. 11. 24), seem to promise that he will be present to Christians as he was to the disciples at his Last Supper. Even the way some of the incidents are told in the Gospels conveys a lively sense of Jesus' presence and attitudes.

If we read the Gospels primarily in a critical way, we are not likely to be encountered by Christ in them. It is, of course, perfectly proper and even highly desirable for the trained New Testament scholar to scrutinize the Gospels with a view to establishing so far as is possible the original text, to interpret the words and incidents in the light of what we know about the Judaism of that time, to apply tests to determine whether a saying attributed to Jesus is likely to be authentic, to distinguish the legendary material which inevitably grew around a spiritual leader in the ancient world from actual historical happenings, and so on. But the alternative is not to be uncritical or fundamentalist. Rather, it is to be open to the spiritual message which is the main concern of a Gospel as distinct from a biography. The amazing thing is that sometimes we do catch the authentic voice of Jesus or recognize his special characteristics in some incident. At such moments, the text comes alive and touches or even transforms the person of the reader. As Archbishop Michael Ramsey showed in his book *The Gospel and the Catholic Church*, the spiritual content of the Gospels only addresses us in the context of the church.

A few sentences back, I said that the words 'Do this for the recalling of me' in the eucharist can be heard almost as a promise of Christ. A New Testament scholar might say, 'These are not original words of Christ, for they appear in only two of the four accounts of the Last Supper, those of Paul and Luke, and they are not in Matthew and Mark.' To this one can only reply, 'So what?' In these early traditions, it is impossible to know exactly what came from Christ and what from the church, and it does not matter. For the church was the community of the risen Christ, dependent on his Spirit and speaking in his name. The church is the Body of Christ, continuing his presence on earth. To quote Michael Ramsey, 'The fact of Christ includes the fact of the Church.'[2] On the specific question of eucharistic origins, he says, 'The dominical origin of the eucharist does not stand or fall with the authenticity of the command to "do this".'[3] The question is much too subtle to be solved by the (always doubtful) results of applying 'objective' tests devised by professedly disinterested researchers. I might also quote here some words of Eric Mascall: 'The theologian is right in demanding objectivity, but objectivity is not to be achieved by pursuing it as an ultimate ideal, with frequent glances out of the corner of the eye for the approbation of the secular scholar. The theologian needs, of course, certain gifts of intellect and a technical training . . . but most of all he needs that feel of the truth, that "knowledge by connaturality" which comes from living as a member of Christ in the Church, which is Christ's body.'[4] Paul speaks of a 'spiritual wisdom and understanding' (Col. 1. 9), and tells us that although people who are concerned only with matters of fact dismiss such spiritual understanding as folly, there are some things that can be only 'spiritually discerned' (I Cor. 2. 14). That which is 'spiritually discerned' cannot be demonstrated by argument, but it is not merely arbitrary. Rather, it may be claimed that spiritual discernment is a seeing in depth, an insight beneath the outward phenomena to their inward constitutive meaning.

These notions are obviously relevant to the question that is at present before our minds, namely, 'How do we know Jesus Christ?' We say he is 'more' than a rabbi, 'more' than a prophet, 'more' than a charismatic teacher of wisdom. What is this 'more'? We say he is 'the Christ, the son of the living God', and therefore more than any ordinary human being. This is not something demonstrable, not an observable fact like, say, the colour of his eyes. As Jesus said to Peter, 'Flesh and blood has not revealed this to you' (Matt. 16. 17). It is something more than appears on the surface level. It is, as I said, something that cannot be demonstrated by scientific method, but nevertheless we must try as far as we can to understand what is at issue here, and at least to satisfy ourselves that we are not wandering into a realm of pure fantasy.

Let us remind ourselves of our starting-point. It was quite minimal, namely, that Jesus of Nazareth did really exist in human history. But this is not quite so minimal as it may appear at first sight. Jesus of Nazareth was a human being, and a human being is like a little world. There is already included in that being an almost infinite range of processes, thoughts, desires, imaginings, emotions, hopes . . . one could extend the list indefinitely. A human being has a body, but is not a mere thing, and not just a living body or animal, but a person who has a claim to be recognized and treated as a person. The distinction between persons and things is absolutely fundamental in human experience, and is reflected in language. Hence, as Buber expressed it, there are two primary words, or two primary combinations of words, I-thou and I-it. He went on to say: 'The primary word I-thou can only be spoken with the whole being. The primary word I-it can never be spoken with the whole being.'[5]

This statement draws attention to two quite different ways of knowing and experiencing, almost to two different worlds. Indeed, the first sentence in Buber's book says that 'to man the world is twofold'. In a sense, we can speak only *to* another person. We can only speak *about* a thing. We can also speak *about* a person, yet even in speaking about a person, there is a different quality in our talk. We do not talk about persons as we do about things.

There are of course borderline cases. We sometimes speak to an animal, but only in a very limited way. We would be very surprised if the animal answered back – there is no conversation. Sometimes we talk to a person or about a person as if he or she were a thing. That would be the case in a society which included slaves, but there is in the modern world an almost universal acceptance that slavery is immoral and an offence to humanity.

So what does it mean to say that the I-thou language is spoken with the whole being, the I-it never with the whole being? Perhaps the fundamental point is the one that has just been mentioned, that in the speaking to another person, there is reciprocity or conversation, and this is impossible with things. We may learn a great deal about things, we do in fact through the sciences have a vast understanding of the material universe in its different aspects, yet in some sense it remains an alien existence and we cannot enter into its processes and experience them from within, as it were. We experience the world of things 'objectively', as something 'out there', to be observed and described. With persons it is quite different. We have a kinship with them, and although no one can enter directly into the thoughts and experiences of another, he assumes that the other has experiences similar to his own. So there is possible here a degree of penetration or participation such as is not possible in one's relation to inanimate things.

Again, one has to say that there are borderline cases. The artist, for example, sees a mountain as more than a mass of rock, and acknowledges, without any sentimental projection of human feelings on to it, its beauty and dignity simply as a mountain. But even so, this is different from the relation of person-to-person.

Buber says that when the word 'thou'[6] is spoken, it is spoken by the whole being of the speaker. I think this is a fair point. When a geologist speaks, as a geologist, of a mountain, he is speaking with that part of his being which is intellectual, cerebral, focussed on the kind of knowledge which we call 'scientific', 'objective' or even 'detached'. But when someone (it may well be the geologist!) is speaking of a friend or to a friend, his words express his whole being, his feelings, his aspirations, everything that belongs to him as a person. He knows and in turn is known in a much fuller, broader sense than is the case in knowing the geological facts of the mountain. Nowadays the prestige of the natural sciences is so great that some people want to reserve words like 'knowing' and 'cognition' for objective knowledge of facts, but I think that some of our most fundamental knowledge is gained from what may be called the total human experience, not just from observation and intellectual analysis. For instance, from the point of view of human self-understanding, perhaps nothing is more important than to become aware of one's own finitude, and by this I do not mean just knowing *about* the fact that a human being and indeed the human race appear to be as insignificant in the universe as the humblest insect is on earth, but to have a genuine existential awareness of one's own finitude. But this awareness, as thinkers from Kierkegaard to Heidegger have shown, is made known to us not through philosophical speculation but through the affective experience of anxiety. If the example I have given seems too negative or pessimistic, it could equally well have been said that the apprehension of finitude inevitably brings with it the apprehension of infinity and that the human person through the experience of transcendence glimpses an infinite horizon.

We know other human beings in various degrees of depth. Buber used the expression 'I-thou' for an intimate relationship in which one may say there is a total or near-total participation of two human beings in each other, something much deeper than knowing a fact, yet something that certainly deserves the name of knowledge, even knowledge in the fullest sense. A fulfilled marriage would be a good example. It is interesting that in an older English usage, the word 'know' was used of the sexual relation: 'And Adam knew Eve his wife, and she conceived . . .' (Gen. 4. 1). But there are many human relationships, some deeper and some less so, in which knowing and being known embrace a wider range of the capacities of the person than the intellect.

Love could be described as a way of knowing. In the example I gave in the preceding paragraph, I cited the case of erotic love. But all kinds of love have a cognitive component. For instance, John's Gospel (written probably by the 'disciple whom Jesus loved') may contain material that is historically less reliable about objective facts than the Synoptic Gospels, but gives a deeper insight into the person of Jesus. To give another example: in the sciences, a student or researcher who, as we say, 'loves' the subject, is more likely to 'notice' things missed by someone who is indifferent.

Simply because he is a person, Jesus Christ has to be known in ways that go beyond the historical data. In fact, there is a word for the special kind of relationship that the Christian has with Christ, the relationship in which he knows Christ, and that word is 'faith'. Faith is drained of its vitality if it is interpreted merely as belief. Certainly, faith will always contain belief, such as the belief, mentioned earlier, that Jesus did really exist as a person in human history, and that the reports of his career in the New Testament are broadly reliable. But faith contains much more than belief, and is a more complicated relationship, with many strands to it. Faith has a different object from belief. We believe propositions, but we have faith in persons. Perhaps the best word to describe such faith is 'commitment', and this is an existential attitude of the whole man or woman. It was through faith in Christ that the first disciples began to perceive the 'more' in him and their understanding of him gradually deepened. There is reciprocity in the relation, as in all interpersonal relations. As the faithful disciple enters into a deeper understanding of Christ, so Christ imparts his own qualities to the disciples, and the latter's life too is deepened. Paul speaks of this remarkable reciprocity in knowing Jesus Christ. As one of those still growing in faith, but looking towards its final goal, he writes: 'Now we see in a mirror dimly, but then face to face; now I know in part, then I shall understand fully, even as I have been fully understood' (I Cor. 13. 12).

Perhaps the highest reach of faith is found in mysticism, which I take to be a kind of total immersion in the divine and therefore perhaps the highest level of knowledge possible for a human person on earth. I hasten to say that I myself am not a mystic. I have admired the river from the banks and dabbled in the shallows, but have never had the courage to plunge into the depths. But I think Paul could well be described as a mystic, and has in fact been so described by the New Testament scholar Adolf Deissmann. He interprets the recurring phrase 'in Christ' in the Pauline letters to mean a mystical relation, and writes about Paul: 'In communion with Christ, he found communion with God; Christ-intimacy was experience and confirmation of God-intimacy. [Paul] was not deified nor was he trans-formed into spirit by the communion nor did he become Christ. But he was transformed by God, he became spiritual and he was one whom Christ possessed and a Christ-bearer.'[7]

Deissmann's characterization of Paul as a mystic has been contested, but I think there can be no doubt in the case of Bonaventure, whose mystical experience of God was, like

Paul's, mediated through the person of Jesus Christ. I mention Bonaventure especially because of the description he gives of the multi-stranded way by which the mystic comes to the knowledge of God. He addresses these words to his readers: 'First, therefore, I invite the reader to the groans of prayer through Christ crucified . . . so that he does not believe that reading is sufficient without unction, speculation without devotion, investigation without wonder, observation without joy, work without piety, knowledge without love, understanding without humility, endeavour without divine grace, reflection as a mirror without divine wisdom.'[8] Bonaventure is there describing a path by which we come to know Jesus as not only Jesus of Nazareth but as Jesus the Christ. We learn something of the 'more' that marks off this truly human Jesus from the mass of mankind. And the reciprocity of the relationship is surely shown in an eminent way in the disciple who was Bonaventure's great hero, St Francis. He was so totally immersed in Christ that he received the stigmata of Christ's wounds. I do not profess to know what these stigmata were, whether physical or spiritual or possibly both, but they set before us as perhaps nothing else could the closeness of the saint's relation to Christ, or, if you prefer, the fullness of his knowledge.

So far I have been arguing that the depth and complexity of a person are such that disinterested reporting of the objective facts of that person's life are insufficient for us to *know* him or her in any depth. Such knowing could only be obtained in a relationship involving the whole person, not just the intellect.

But now a further problem arises. How is it possible to have a personal contact with a human being of the past, especially the distant past? Are we not confined in such a case to knowledge by description, while knowledge by acquaintance is denied us, or is at best reduced to a few items when the historical data come alive, as we say, and we hear the voice or get a glimpse of the inner life? That is perhaps what we would have to say if Jesus or any other person were an isolated individual. We ourselves do happen to live in an age of intense individualism. This is part of our inheritance from the Enlightenment, and it is one of the least admirable parts of that inheritance. It seems to have been in the mind of Don Cupitt when he wrote that 'when we use the name Jesus we designate first and foremost the individual who answered to that name in Galilee, and of whom a certain minimal description established by historians is for the most part true'.[9] Recognizing that some things have been attributed to Jesus which may have been added by the early Christian community, he declares that 'what is said of Jesus must be something that can plausibly be said of the historical individual who answered to that name'.[10]

I think it must be firmly replied to this that when we speak of a person, though indeed we probably have in mind some particular named individual, that individual is only a person in so far as he or she stands in relation to other individuals. The autonomous isolated I is something less than a person. To use a phrase which can be found in Buber but was actually in use at least from the time of Feuerbach, 'There is no I without a thou'. A community is made up of persons, but equally these persons are formed by the community. The Enlightenment theory of the social contract, found in Rousseau and many other philosophers of that period, the theory namely that autonomous individuals had come together and contracted each to surrender part of his autonomy in return for the security and other benefits of living in a community is quite false. The human person is, from the beginning, a relational being, bound up with other human persons in what is sometimes called a web of life. Heidegger expressed this by saying that the human being is essentially a being-with-others, just as he or she is also a being-in-the-world.[11] If the contexts of a world of things and a society of persons are removed, I do not know just what would be left, but I do not believe it would be a person.

The idea that a person is constituted through his or her relations to other persons has been applied to Jesus Christ by a number of theologians in different traditions. Among Roman Catholic theologians, Jean Galot has laid great stress on the relational character of Christ's person.[12] Rudolf Bultmann may have been the originator of the expression 'Christ-event' to indicate that at the origin of Christianity there is not simply an individual, Jesus of Nazareth, but a social reality, Jesus together with those related to him in the community of faith. All this has been spelled out more fully by the American New Testament scholar, John Knox. He tells us that the 'Christ-event' includes 'the personality, life and teaching of Jesus, the response of loyalty he awakened, his death, his resurrection, the receiving of the Spirit, the faith with which the Spirit was received, the coming into being of the Church'.[13] This is obviously a very complex reality, a whole system of relations. But it is simply an expansion of the claim that we met in Michael Ramsey – 'The fact of Christ includes the fact of the Church'.[14] Jesus is not simply an isolated individual, whatever that might mean, but as Jesus the Christ he stands at the centre of a whole world of relationships, reaching back into Israel and the voices of the prophets, reaching out among his contemporaries from whom he called his apostles and disciples, and reaching forward into the time of the church, including our own time. Jesus is the inspirer and centre of this whole movement. The incarnation is not just the coming of God in an individual man but the creation of a new humanity.

So we see how it might be claimed that even in the twentieth and subsequent centuries it is possible to have a personal relationship to Christ, even leaving aside for the present any appeal to resurrection. Our assurance of the reality of Christ and of his saving power does not rest primarily on the testimony of the New Testament witnesses, but on the present experience of Christ in his church. We ourselves have been caught up in the Christ-event, which is still going on. It is in this community, with its proclamation of the word and its sacraments, that the person of Jesus Christ still impinges upon us. Countless sermons have been preached, telling the faithful that they must be disciples at first hand, not disciples at second hand. That is possible because Jesus Christ is still present in the continuing Christ-event, the living community which he created and which has gone on for almost two thousand years.

We talk of 'apostolic succession', and by that we mean a transmission of the Spirit of Christ from one generation to another through a living community of persons. Though we usually think of this succession as peculiarly associated with the bishops who have responsibility for its orderly transmission, yet in a broad sense the whole church stands in this succession.

At this point a critical question may arise for us. When we speak of an 'event', we are usually thinking of a happening that is limited in space and time. It might be the event of a day, such as the coming of the Spirit on the Day of Pentecost, or an event spread over several years, for instance, the

Second World War or the Second Vatican Council. But is it legitmate to use the word 'event' of a series of happenings that have gone on for two thousand years, or more if we trace its roots back into the history of Israel, and which still has before it an indefinite future stretching ahead? If we are justified in speaking of the Christ-event, then we seem to be talking of a unique event, a cosmic event, transcending all the events of human history.

We began this chapter by asking, 'How do we know Christ?' We have, I think, seen that when we set aside the positivistic prohibitions that have been characteristic of the twentieth century, we can indeed attain to a knowledge of Christ, not only the historical knowledge that comes to us through written documents and research into them, but a knowledge also of that mysterious 'more' or overplus in Christ that distinguishes him from the rest of the human race. We have seen that as the centre and source of what we could only call a cosmic event, he himself has a cosmic significance. Nothing that we have seen infringes his genuine humanity, but we have been pointed towards a metaphysical significance in him, and that is the theme we shall take up in the final chapter.

6

The Metaphysical Christ

'Jesus Christ is the goal of everything, and the centre to which everything tends. He who knows him knows the reason of all things.'[1] These words were written by the mathematician and philosopher, Blaise Pascal, in the seventeenth century, and the first time I read them, many years ago, my reaction was decidedly negative. Surely, I thought, a claim like this is going away beyond what is reasonable. Is Christ really the centre of everything and explanation of everything? If one claims this for Christ in this modern age, is it not more likely to turn people away from Christianity than to attract them? Is this not an altogether dogmatic claim, which simply skims over all the serious questions that arise in human minds, and ignores all the intellectual labours of generations of scientists and historians, and all the spiritual strivings and achievements of men and women in non-Christian religions and cultures? Even today, I shrink somewhat from the claim, especially when it is stated as boldly as we find it in Pascal. It is certainly a claim so inclusive, so overwhelming, that it needs to be teased out and carefully examined before any reasonable conscientious person could accept it. But suppose we do try to tease it out and examine it, might we find that we are inexorably driven toward acceptance? Is this claim not implicit in Christianity? We say, using the apparently simple formula of Paul, 'God was in Christ, reconciling the world to himself' (II Cor. 5. 19), and when we say that there is 'something more' in Jesus Christ which gives him his distinctiveness, then perhaps if we are prepared to explore these claims as far as we can, we shall have to make the confession that Pascal made, though we might wish to phrase it in ways that would seem less dogmatic, and would be less abrasive to persons who do think that Pascal was going too far too fast.

If we say 'God was in Christ', then we are claiming that there was or is something transcendent in Jesus Christ, something that goes beyond a historical human life, something that is eternal. At the beginning of this book,[2] I quoted Bonhoeffer's question, 'Who is Jesus Christ for us today?', but in and through Jesus Christ men and women have had glimpses of a reality that is indeed the 'centre of everything' and is not just 'for us today' but is for everyone at all times. The Letter to the Hebrews contains a sentence just as breathtaking as Pascal's: 'Jesus Christ is the same yesterday and today and for ever' (Heb. 13. 8). It would be wrong to say that there is merely an eternal component in Jesus Christ, for that would seem to be splitting him in two, and in any case the eternal component would, so to speak, swallow up the temporal component, as indeed it was allowed to do in some idealist philosophies, with the result that Jesus Christ becomes simply an ideal or an archetype, deprived of his human and historical actuality and therefore of his significance for the human condition.

With some reluctance, I have entitled the present chapter 'The Metaphysical Christ'. I say, 'with some reluctance', because the word 'metaphysical' has been unfashionable among many philosophers during most of the twentieth century, though we should not forget that a significant minority have continued to champion the metaphysical enterprise, and have claimed that its relinquishment has signalled a lapse from seriousness. I do not believe that human beings will ever give up asking questions about God, the destiny of our race, and any other so-called ultimate questions. Certainly the prohibitions of philosophers will not deter them, for these questions are too deeply rooted in our very humanity. But metaphysics, in the strict sense, was the attempt to answer these questions out of the resources of human reasoning and experience alone. As I argued in the previous chapter, I think that cognition has a broader base and more diverse sources than many contemporary philosophers allow. Some such belief was held also by Pascal, and underlies his claim that Jesus Christ is the centre to which everything tends. He himself rejected the metaphysical attempts to prove the existence of God,[3] but at the same time he claimed that 'we know the truth not only by means of the reason, but also by means of the heart, and it is in the latter way that we know first principles . . . The heart has its reasons, which reason does not know.'[4] By the 'heart', he appears to mean those modes of understanding and spiritual insight which I attempted to describe in the preceding chapter. Admittedly, Pascal was a pre-Enlightenment, or at any rate, early Enlightenment figure – he died in 1662 – but in his day he was a leader in the fields of mathematics and physics, and knew both the strengths and the limitations of rational thought. So when I talk of the metaphysical Christ, I do not mean a conception of Christ based on abstract metaphysical argument, but the ultimate or transcendent characteristics of Christ, discoverable not by historical research or mere observation, but by what Paul called 'spiritual discernment'.

Pascal's bold claim for Jesus Christ has been repeated by some Christian thinkers of the twentieth century, notably by Dietrich Bonhoeffer. This may be surprising, for, as we have already noted, it was Bonhoeffer who asked the question, 'Who is Jesus Christ for us today?', and such a question might be understood as pointing in the direction of a relativism. But although Bonhoeffer was politically a radical who actively opposed the Nazi regime in Germany, he was theologically a quite conservative Lutheran. Like Pascal, he did not believe that abstract metaphysical argument could bring us to an understanding of God or Christ, but he was willing to have Christian beliefs teased out and examined, and more than that, to have them tested in the real situations of life and, eventually, death.

About twenty years before he asked his question about the meaning of Jesus Christ for the people of the twentieth century, he had given a course of lectures on christology. These were not published until after his death at the hands of the Nazis in 1945, but there is no evidence that his views had changed in that time. Indeed, it seems that they had become more firm in the course of the meditations in which he had engaged during his imprisonment. The actual year in which he gave these lectures was 1933, a very significant year in European history, because it was in January of that year that Adolf Hitler came to power in Germany. He founded the Third Reich, which was to be the new power centre of the world and was designed to last for a thousand years. It may have been in conscious opposition to this new centre of power that Bonhoeffer made the theme of 'Christ the centre' a leading idea in his christology. When the lectures were published, the English edition published in London was entitled simply *Christology*, but the American edition was given the more informative and significant title, *Christ the Centre*.[5] It is quite possible that Bonhoeffer's use of the 'centre' motif was a deliberate echo of Pascal.

In his introductory remarks, Bonhoeffer makes a point which seems obvious, yet is so obvious that we usually overlook it. His point is that if Christ is the Logos or Word of God, as Christians claim, then christology is the science of the Word, or, to put it succinctly, christology is logology, the logos concerning logos, and therefore, says Bonhoffer, the 'crown of learning'.[6] To this quite dramatic beginning of his course, Bonhoeffer at once adds two clarifications.

The first is that the logos which is the subject of logology is not human discourse. I suppose the right word for the study of human discourse would be 'logic'. But the logos of christology/logology is the Word of God, that is to say, a transcendent Word. This is not man's own word, but the Word that has come to man from God in the person of Jesus Christ, of whom Bonhoeffer says, 'This man is transcendent'. So the Word is not merely an idea, but a person. Bonhoeffer may at this point have been distancing himself from German idealist philosophers, especially Kant, for whom the 'life well-pleasing to God' was an archetype discoverable by reason and needing, so Kant claimed, no empirical exemplar in history. When, however, Kant seeks to spell out the content of this archetype, it seems clear that he had in fact based it on the historical career of Jesus Christ, for he writes: 'This idea of a humanity pleasing to God (hence of such moral perfection as is possible to an earthly being who is subject to wants and inclinations) we can represent to ourselves only as the idea of a person who would be willing, not merely to discharge all human duties and to spread about him goodness as widely as possible by precept and example, but even, though tempted by the greatest allurements, to take upon himself every affliction, up to the most ignominious death, for the good of the world and even of his enemies.'[7] Surely we must here agree with

Bonhoeffer as against Kant and other anti-historical idealists that what Kant has so eloquently and concisely described is not just an idea, but, as Christians believe, the concrete reality of the life of Christ.

The second point that Bonhoeffer makes about christology is that because of its claim to be *the discipline par excellence* and the centre of its sphere, christology stands alone. There is no proof by which it can demonstrate the transcendence of its subject. This is an important point and somewhat qualifies the notion that, as the centre of everything, Christ and the study of Christ somehow supersedes all other sciences. Bonhoeffer is saying that there is no competition, no rivalry. Christology is not, for instance, in competition with a disinterested historical investigation of the life of Jesus, for in christology the discussion has moved into quite another sphere. But if we are willing to broaden our ideas of what may or may not count as knowing, as was discussed in the previous chapter, if we are willing to allow weight to such experiences as faith and mysticism, then we can accept that a transcendent Word has indeed come to us in Jesus Christ. It may be noted here that Bonhoeffer, like many Lutheran theologians, himself rejects mysticism (very probably from a failure to understand what it is), but he would think of faith as sufficient to provide the presupposition for christology, which would then be a case of faith seeking understanding.

Bonhoeffer expands the notion of Christ as centre under three headings: Christ is the centre of human existence, the centre of history and the mediator between God and nature. Bonhoeffer's lectures had to be reconstructed from the notes taken by students, and one gets the impression at this point that there has been severe abridgement, so that the sequence of thought is not always clear. He insists that the three points cannot be demonstrated because they concern matters in which proof is not possible. I comment briefly on these three points.

As the centre of human existence, Christ may be considered as the fulfilment of God's project in the creation of the human race (echoes of Schleiermacher!). He is at once the norm against which humanity is to be judged, and the firstfruits of a new humanity. 'Christ as the centre of human existence means that he is man's judgment and his justification.'[8] Here Bonhoeffer comes close to cutting himself free from all the ancient wrangles over justification that have embroiled Lutherans, and likewise the inappropriate legal imagery that was employed by theologians. If we are sometimes inclined to wonder whether the creation of the human race was a mistake, considering all the sin and evil that human beings have produced, Bonhoeffer seems to be saying, 'No! the experiment of humanity is justified by the representative man, the true man, Jesus Christ'.

As the centre of history, Christ is again being designated in a way that is not demonstrable. So it is no argument against the claim to say that one cannot fix a date for the centre of history or even know whether it makes sense to look for a centre of history. The centrality of Christ for history is not quantitative but qualitative. Bonhoeffer thought of history as the way that lies between promise and fulfilment. The very act of creation concealed within itself the promise of fulfilment, and Christ's coming was the decisive moment in the fulfilling of the promise. Nowadays Christians, in their desire not to offend members of other religions or of no religion by dating events BC (Before Christ) or AD (In the year of the Lord), sometimes use the conventions BCE (Before Common Era) and CE (Common Era). However, this way of talking only serves to emphasize the universal or cosmic significance of Jesus Christ. The change in the eras was and is a change for the whole human race, and this seems to be tacitly acknowledged by the adoption worldwide of the Christian calendar, whatever descriptions are used for the eras.

Bonhoeffer's third point is that Jesus Christ is the mediator between God and nature. The published version of the lectures contains only the barest summary of this point, and it is not entirely clear. There seem to have been two ideas in his mind. One was the idea of a cosmic fall, the belief that not only the human race but the whole creation is fallen and infected by sin. This belief has appeared from time to time in the history of theology, and perhaps today it has become more credible as we become aware of the extent to which human exploitation of nature has polluted not only the planet but even the surrounding space. The other idea in Bonhoeffer's mind tends to balance the first one and gives a more affirmative picture. From Jesus Christ there has been derived a sacramental theology, by which material things from the old creation are brought into the new creation and given a new significance as means of grace.

Enough has been said to show that Bonhoeffer in our own century was setting forth Christ as the centre in the spirit of Pascal. He had in fact planned to give some further lectures in his course on the theme of 'The Eternal Christ', but the end of the semester came before they could be delivered and, as often happens, the professor was excused from dealing with the most difficult issues in the course. If these lectures were ever written, or even sketched out, they have not been discovered.

The Swiss theologian, Heinrich Ott says, 'The question, "What is reality?" could be called the peculiar theme of all [Bonhoeffer's] thinking.'[9] And one would have to say that for him, 'reality' is Jesus Christ. This is what I mean by the 'metaphysical' Christ. In the words of the Scottish liturgy, as revised in 1982 and reminiscent of patristic theology, '[Christ] is the Word, existing beyond time, both source and final purpose, bringing to wholeness all that is made'.

From a very different vantage-point, the Jesuit Pierre Teilhard de Chardin arrived at similar ideas about christology, and made metaphysical claims for Christ no less far-reaching than those of Bonhoeffer. He saw Jesus Christ against the background of evolution, and went so far as to claim that 'the exclusive task of the world is the physical incorporation of the faithful into the Christ who is of God'.[10] Like Bonhoeffer, he could think of even the material creation as embraced in the process of 'christification'.

Even when we have tried to open up and explore these highly exalted views of Christ, from Pascal to Bonhoeffer and Teilhard, they may still seem to us to be extravagant. We may feel a measure of uneasiness, wondering if the claims that have been made are not too dogmatic, and whether they may not be too cavalier in their dismissal of persons who for one reason or another have not been able to see Jesus Christ quite in these terms. I think it can be conceded that some christocentric theologians may have introduced their understanding of Christ in too abrupt and isolated a manner, without regard to the relations of Jesus Christ to Israel, to the church, even to the general body of mankind, relations which we saw to be essential to the personal being of Jesus Christ, when we discussed the idea of a 'Christ-event'.[11] Jesus Christ is never just an individual – he is Jesus the Jew in relation to Israel, Jesus the Lord in relation to the church, Jesus the authentic human person in relation to the human race. Even in relation to God, in

Christian thought he is the Second Person of the Trinity, and if we tear him from that context, we run the risk of what has been called a 'unitarianism of the Second Person' or even 'Jesusolatry'. The theologians we have been considering did not deny these various relationships, but in their anxiety to exalt Christ, they may (with the exception of Teilhard) have obscured the personal context and made him an anomaly, a 'rock in the sky' as was sometimes said by some of Barth's critics about his christomonistic tendencies.

Actually, as I hinted earlier, the Christian faith itself, when we seriously consider its implications, may drive us to make the highest claims for Christ, But if we want to commend Christ in a secular world, and even if we want to be intellectually honest and to set at ease any traces of embarrassment we may feel in the face of the claim 'Christ is the centre of everything', we may think there is wisdom in supplying an adequate context for this claim.

Thus, for instance, one reads in Berdyaev, 'man is not a fragmentary part of the world, but contains the whole riddle of the universe and the solution of it'.[12] This statement expresses an idea that has been around since ancient times, the idea that man is a microcosm, that all the levels of being that are present in the cosmos are present in the human being – the matter that composes our bodies and obeys the laws of physics and chemistry, the biological constitution of our bodies which makes them organic unities in which the whole and the parts are reciprocally unified, our faculties of perception and sentience which we have in common with other living things, the higher capacities for thought and will and personal relations which are peculiarly human, and which relate us to God himself. Every human being is therefore a little world, summing up in himself or herself the ingredients of the cosmos. We could even say that with the appearance of the human race on this planet the cosmos has come to speech and conscious understanding. For billions of years, there was building up the possibility of such a being as man, and at some point it did indeed emerge on earth. Perhaps similar beings have emerged elsewhere – we do not know, and it would make no difference to our discussion. This reminder of the constitution of the human race does not in any way diminish the claims made for Christ, but it does supply a context which makes these claims more intelligible and less arbitrary. For if the divine or the transcendent is going to appear anywhere on this earth, it will not be (*pace* William of Ockham) in a stone or an ass (unless in a very obscure way) but in a human being, made in the divine image and likeness (Gen. 1. 26). If Jesus Christ is the new Adam, the true man, then one must go on and conclude with Paul that he is 'the image of the invisible God' (Col. 1. 15). To remember that the whole human race was created in the image and likeness of God, however disfigured that image may have become, is in no sense to diminish the status of the representative man, Jesus Christ, but it is a help towards making the mystery of incarnation more intelligible.

However, I do not think that theologians will ever attain to a full understanding of incarnation. Ideas like incarnation, resurrection, atonement, lie at the very frontier of understanding. God alone, seeing things from the divine side, can have a full understanding of his own acts. From the human side, we can understand only in part, and even so we have to help ourselves out by the use of myth, metaphor, paradox and other figures of speech. Even Jesus Christ, as we have seen,[13] did not have omniscience and had to grow in knowledge and submit in faith, as in the poignant episode of Gethsemane.

Nevertheless, we have to seek the best understanding possible, and there is one further exercise that may help us in this. We have been engaged in a theological enterprise which began from the basic indisputable fact that approximately two thousand years ago there was living in Palestine a man named Jesus of Nazareth who became the centre of what we call the 'Christ-event', a vast and still expanding network of relationships and happenings. From its obscure origins, this event has come more and more to influence our world, and may finally embrace it completely, as in the vision of the future presented by Teilhard. So let us go back and think again of the course of this cosmic movement that has brought us all the way from the 'marginal Jew', as he has been called, to the 'metaphysical Christ'. We set off from the human Jesus and we end with the divine Christ, yet we say that these two are one. There is a continuous path from the start to the finish. It has not been a purely intellectual argument that has brought us along this way, but an openness to the total Christian experience of Jesus. We have recognized that there is an implicit cognitive content in such religious experiences as repentance, the sense of finitude, the awareness of sin and likewise of transcendence, conscience and the sense of moral obligation, faith, mysticism and so on, all the areas of experience that might be summed up in the Pauline phrases 'spiritual discernment' and 'wisdom of God'. These do not displace rational judgment, but supplement, deepen and enlarge it. I think our theological reflections have followed a course which is in the main parallel to the experience of the first Christians. What they learned in their first-hand experience of Jesus we can replicate in our theological meditation, yet this is not a second-hand experience, for we ourselves are part of the continuing Christ-event. Looking back, then, to the events of Christ's life, can we see the gradual emergence in him and a corresponding recognition among his followers, of the 'something more', as I have been calling it, the something more that makes the difference between the devout Jew at the beginning of the story and the metaphysical Christ at the end?

Perhaps the first glimmer that we get is the incident, recorded only by Luke, of the teenage Jesus' strange behaviour when he slips away from his parents and goes to the Temple to listen to the doctors and to ask them questions. It shows that even in the so-called 'hidden years' of his boyhood, his divine vocation was stirring within him. A conscious commitment to this vocation followed at his baptism, as narrated by the evangelists. Later, a major event was the recognition of Jesus as Messiah or Christ (Mark 8. 27–30). Mark places this in the middle of his ministry, some modern scholars argue that such recognition came only after the death and resurrection, but the dating does not matter very much. The point is that at some time the disciples recognized Jesus as Messiah, the anointed one sent by God to deliver the people. Just what was meant by calling Jesus the 'Christ' is also debatable, but it was an important first step toward acknowledging that there was 'something more' in this man, he was not just another prophet or rabbi or charismatic teacher.

In the next chapter of Mark's Gospel there is a further incident which carries on and deepens the revelation of Jesus' significance – the transfiguration. He is transfigured before the inner circle of disciples, his garments glisten. There is seen in this man a divine glory and a voice is heard: 'This is my beloved Son; listen to him' (Mark 9. 2–8). It is a legendary story, but testifies to a new depth or new glory perceived by the disciples in Jesus, a glory going beyond that of messiahship. Some commentators have seen it as an anticipation of the resurrection. Could we say that it was a numinous moment in their experience, briefly revealing something eternal and indestructible in Jesus, the disciples' first glimpse of the eternal Word, the metaphysical Christ?

Events move on quickly to the passion and crucifixion. Here we must turn especially to John's Gospel. I have from time to time used the expression 'absolute paradox' for the mystery of the God-man. John sees that paradox most clearly in the cross. He tells us that Jesus said to his disciples, 'I, when I am lifted up from the earth, will draw all men to myself'; and by way of explanation, John adds the words, 'He said this to show by what death he was to die' (John 12. 32–33). John does not need to tell any subsequent story of an ascension into heaven – the death on the cross *is* the ascension of Jesus, the manifestation of the glory that he shared with the Father, the exaltation and lifting up from the earth. For in this, John, the 'beloved disciple', saw the divine love humanly expressed. This is the 'absolute paradox' in its strongest form. What further glory could there be after this? In John's words, 'We have seen his glory, the glory as of the only begotten of the Father' (John 1. 14).

However, the Synoptic Gospels tend to find the glory of Jesus in his resurrection. They seem to say that this is the moment when his provenance from the Father is fully and finally revealed. But in the Christian tradition, crucifixion and resurrection are inseparable. However, just as I said that I have sometimes felt embarrassed by the forthright declaration that Jesus Christ is the centre of everything, so nowadays many Christian preachers and teachers feel embarrassed in speaking of the resurrection of Jesus. They know and accept Paul's claim that 'If Christ has not been raised, then our preaching is in vain, and your faith is in vain' (I Cor. 15. 14). Yet they know also that in our sceptical age people just do not believe in the possibility of resurrection, at least, as the word is commonly understood.

At this point, the theologian or preacher has to be honest and to admit that we do not know enough about God's action or even about the mystery of our own humanity to be able to explain what happened on Easter Day. The Gospels themselves pass over the actual event in silence. They bring us to that moment on the Friday when the body of the Lord is laid in the tomb. Then there is a gap in the story. The narration starts up again on the Sunday with the finding of an empty tomb. On any reasonable expectation, the story ought to have ended on the Friday, but it started up again and has gone on ever since. The disciples had fled and scattered when Jesus was arrested, but they came together again and the history of the church began. The enemies of Jesus had calculated well. They thought that if they could take out the leader of the new movement, there was no one among his followers able to continue it, and it would simply collapse. But in fact, they had miscalculated, for the story did not end with the death and burial. The story showed a different pattern, which we may schematize as burial-interval-continuation. It is interesting to note that exactly this pattern appears in a mention of Christian origins, written by the Roman historian Tacitus about sixty years after the crucifixion. Tacitus, who called Christianity a 'deadly superstition', says that after the execution of Christ, it was 'checked for a moment, then broke out again, not only in Judaea, the first source of the evil, but also in the city [of Rome]'.[14] His threefold pattern of check-interval-renewal exactly parallels the pattern of the evangelists, and is an unconscious testimony to the strange turn of events which Christians claimed was due to the resurrection of

Jesus. Although I have the greatest admiration for John Meier's magnificent study, perhaps he does less than justice to Tacitus when he writes, 'If Tacitus represents an independent source – which is doubtful – all he gives us is an added confirmation of Jesus' execution by Pontius Pilate in Judea during the reign of Tiberius.'[15] I suggest that he may be giving us quite unaware the information that after the crucifixion there was a turn of the tide which the disciples claimed was due to the 'resurrection' of Jesus.

This is not the place for an extended discussion of 'resurrection', but some brief remarks are needed, since I have not discussed the topic earlier in the book. There may have been several reasons for the rise of the belief that Jesus had been raised from the dead. The reports of an empty tomb may have been one; visions of the risen Lord granted to some of the disciples may have been another; perhaps a pondering of the Hebrew prophets was a third (so Schillebeeckx). My own belief is that a continuing sense of the presence of Christ, together with meditation on such events of his life as the transfiguration (a kind of anticipation of the resurrection) and above all the sacrifice of Calvary, had convinced the disciples that in Jesus Christ they had indeed beheld the glory of the Father. This process of a growing awareness of the glory of God in Christ had reached its climax at the cross, the revelation of the 'pure unbounded love' of God in the Crucified One. The eternal life of God himself, untouched by death and imperishable, had met them in the man from Nazareth. Their immediate reaction to his arrest was to flee and scatter. But the reality of Christ drew them back. In the interval following the death of Christ they came to know in a new depth 'Christ and the power of his resurrection' (Phil. 3. 10).

Perhaps the last item in the conception of the metaphysical Christ is the question of pre-existence, the first item in the story but the last in our understanding of the story. If Christ lived on in the power of God after his death, must he not be, like God himself, without beginning as well as without end? As early as the Pauline epistles, we see beginnings of trinitarian (or binitarian) doctrine and its relation to the doctrine of Christ. 'For us there is one God, the Father, from whom are all things and for whom we exist, and one Lord, Jesus Christ, through whom are all things and through whom we exist' (I Cor. 8. 6). Jesus Christ is the expressive being of God, the Word in whom the Source of Godhood, the Father, has come out of his hiddenness and silence to form a creation. In that creation, the Word has found fullest expression in a human life. We must not suppose that Christ pre-existed in the sense of waiting like an actor in the wings for the cue when he would step on to the stage of history 'in the fullness of time'. But it does mean that from the beginning Christ the incarnate Word was there in the counsels of God, and even his humanity, like the humanity of us all, was taking shape in the long ages of cosmic evolution. There is nothing in all this that offends reason, though it certainly goes beyond what reason can reach; and there is nothing in it either that would deny that the divine Word has manifested itself beyond the human life of Jesus, in nature, in history, in the non-Christian religions. But for the Christian, he remains, as Pascal claimed, the centre of everything. This is the absolute paradox – that this humble crucified man is also the eternal Word of God.

Notes

1. *The Absolute Paradox*

1. D. Bonhoeffer, *Letters and Papers from Prison*, Revised Edition, SCM Press, London and Macmillan, New York 1967, p. 139.
2. P. Berger, *A Rumour of Angels*, Doubleday, Garden City, NY 1969 and Allen Lane, London 1970, p. 36.
3. Ibid., p. 50.
4. K. Rahner, *Theological Investigations*, Vol. 1, Darton, Longman and Todd, London 1961, p. 149.
5. S. Kierkegaard, *Philosophical Fragments*, Princeton University Press 1936, p. 29.
6. The expression used by John Meier in the title of his monumental study of Jesus (see Chapter 6, n. 15).
7. A. Schweitzer, *The Quest of the Historical Jesus*, A. & C. Black, London 1954, p. 397.
8. T. M. Lindsay, *A History of the Reformation*, T. & T. Clark, Edinburgh 1909, Vol. 1, p. 194.
9. D. Bonhoeffer, *Christ the Centre*, Harper and Row, New York 1966, p. 71.
10. Ibid., p. 88.
11. L. Wittgenstein, *Tractatus Logico-Philosophicus*, Kegan Paul, London 1933, p. 187.

12. S. Kierkegaard, *Training in Christianity*, Princeton University Press 1941, p. 28.

2. *The Humanity of Christ*

1. Clement of Alexandria, *Stromateis*, 6, 9.
2. F.D.E. Schleiermacher, *The Christian Faith*, T. & T. Clark, Edinburgh 1928, p. 99.
3. Leo the Great, *Tome*, 4.
4. Leo did not distinguish between 'nature' and 'person'. See below, pp. 54–5.
5. Some scholars believe that the language should be taken as singular rather than plural, but the textual evidence seems to point definitely to the plural.
6. K. Barth, *Church Dogmatics*, Vol. 1/2, T. & T. Clark, Edinburgh 1956, p. 177.
7. Ibid., p. 182.
8. K. Barth, *Church Dogmatics*, Vol. 4/4 (fragment), T. & T. Clark, Edinburgh 1969, p. 9.
9. R. Bultmann, in C. Braaten and R. Harrisville (eds.), *The Historical Jesus and the Kerygmatic Christ*, Abingdon Press, Nashville 1964, p. 23.
10. Ray Brown, *Jesus, God and Man*, Bruce Publications, Milwaukee 1967, pp. 104–5.

3. *Two Traditional Ideas Evaluated*

1. A. Harnack, *History of Dogma*, Vol. 4, Williams & Norgate, London 1898, p. 336.
2. R.V. Sellers, *The Council of Chalcedon*, SPCK, London 1961, p. 203.
3. A. Grillmeier, *Christ and Christian Tradition*, Vol. 1, Mowbray, London 1975, p. 544.

4. J. Macquarrie, *In Search of Humanity*, SCM Press, London 1982, p. 14.

5. The Greek text of Cyril's letters is in C.A. Heurtley, *De Fide et Symbolo*, Oxford 1889, with a translation in the companion volume, *On Faith and the Creeds*, Oxford 1886.

6. Apollinarius, as quoted by J.N.D. Kelly, *Early Christian Doctrine*, A. & C. Black, London 1968, p. 292.

7. Gregory of Nazianzus, *Ep.* 101.

8. See above, pp. 40–1.

9. See John Knox, *The Humanity and Divinity of Christ*, Cambridge University Press 1967, p. 47.

10. A. Grillmeier, *Christ and Christian Tradition*, Vol. 2/1, Mowbray, Oxford 1987, p. 336.

11. See above, p. 45.

12. H.M. Relton, *A Study in Christology*, SPCK, London 1917, pp. 147–8.

13. A. Grillmeier, *Christ and Christian Tradition*, Vol. 2/2, Mowbray, London 1995.

14. Ibid.

15. J. Meyendorff, *Christ in Eastern Christian Thought*, Corpus Books, Washington 1969, p. 65.

4. A Critique of Adoptionism

1. John Knox, *The Humanity and Divinity of Christ*, Cambridge University Press, 1967, pp. 7–8.

2. Ibid., pp. 9–10.

3. J. Macquarrie, *Jesus Christ in Modern Thought*, SCM Press, London and Trinity Press International, Philadelphia 1990, pp. 55–9.

4. See above, p. 51.

5. Knox, *Humanity and Divinity of Christ* (n. 1), p. 5.

6. Eusebius, *Ecclesiastical History*, vii, 30. Fragments of his teaching are in *A New Eusebius*, ed. J. Stevenson, rev. W. Frend, SPCK, London 1957, 261–2.

7. E. Brunner, *The Mediator*, Lutterworth Press, London 1934, p. 276.

8. J. Macquarrie, 'Christianity without Incarnation? Some Critical Comments', slightly revised review from *Theology*, 1977, in Michael Green, ed., *The Truth of God Incarnate*, Hodder & Stoughton, London 1977, p. 143.

9. E.L. Mascall, *Theology and the Gospel of Christ*, SPCK, London 1977, p. 130.

10. Knox, *Humanity and Divinity of Christ* (n.1), p. 17.

11. Ibid., p. 56.

12. K. Rahner, *Theological Investigations*, Vol. 1, Darton, Longman and Todd, London 1961, p. 155.

13. Mascall, *Theology and the Gospel of Christ* (n.9), p. 121.

14. N. Pittenger, *The Word Incarnate*, Harper and Row, New York 1959, p. 85.

15. J.A.T. Robinson, *The Human Face of God*, SCM Press, London 1973, p. 197.

16. Macquarrie, *Jesus Christ in Modern Thought* (n.3), p. 171.

17. F.D.E. Schleiermacher, *The Christian Faith*, T. & T. Clark, Edinburgh 1928, p. 374.

18. Knox, *Humanity and Divinity of Christ* (n.1), p. 113.

19. Rahner, *Theological Investigations*, Vol. 1 (n.12), p. 184.

5. *How Do We Know Jesus Christ?*

1. Bertrand Russell, *Mysticism and Logic*, Longmans Green, London 1918, pp. 209–32.

2. A.M. Ramsey, *The Gospel and the Catholic Church*, Longmans Green, London 1936, p. 34.

3. Ibid., p. 99.

4. E.L. Mascall, *Theology and the Gospel of Christ*, SPCK, London 1977, p. 35.
5. Martin Buber, *I and Thou*, Scribner, New York 1958, p. 3.
6. Ibid.
7. A. Deissmann, *Paul: A Religious and Social Study*, Hodder & Stoughton, London 1926, p. 153.
8. Bonaventure, *The Soul's Journey into God*, SPCK 1978, p. 55.
9. D. Cupitt, in M. Goulder (ed.), *Incarnation and Myth*, SCM Press, London 1979, p. 32.
10. Ibid., p. 33.
11. M. Heidegger, *Being and Time*, SCM Press, London 1962, pp. 153ff.
12. Jean Galot's christology is expounded in *La Personne du Christ*, 1969, and *Vers une nouvelle christologie*, 1971, both books published by Duculot, Gembloux, Belgium.
13. John Knox, *The Church and the Reality of Christ*, Harper & Row, New York 1962, p. 23.
14. See above, p. 86.

6. The Metaphysical Christ

1. Blaise Pascal, *Pensées*, Garnier-Flammarion, Paris 1973, No. 17, p. 48.
2. See above, p. 10.
3. Pascal, Pensées (n. 1), No. 381, p. 136.
4. Ibid., Nos. 214, 224, pp. 90. 92.
5. D. Bonhoeffer, *Christ the Centre*, Harper and Row, New York 1966, p. 28.
6. Ibid.
7. Immanuel Kant, *Religion within the Limits of Reason Alone*, Harper Torchbooks 1960, p. 55.

8. Bonhoeffer, *Christ the Centre* (n. 5).
9. Heinrich Ott, *Reality and Faith*, Lutterworth Press, London 1971, p. 46.
10. P. Teilhard de Chardin, *The Future of Man*, Harper and Row, New York and Collins, London 1964, p. 318.
11. See above, pp. 95–6.
12. N. Berdyaev, *The Destiny of Man*, Harper Torchbooks, New York 1960, p. 45.
13. See above, pp. 39–40.
14. Tacitus, *Annals 15*, 44.
15. J. Meier, *A Marginal Jew*, Doubleday, New York and London 1991, Vol. 1, p. 140.

Index